Standing Firm Throughout My Healing Journey

Donna Jones

ISBN 978-1-64299-510-7 (paperback)
ISBN 978-1-64299-511-4 (digital)

Christian Faith Publishing, Inc.
832 Park Avenue
Meadville, PA 16335
www.christianfaithpublishing.com

Printed in the United States of America

CONTENTS

INTRODUCTION

My incredible journey with God began the day I was born; however, I didn't know or realize it until my life took a dramatic twist starting in 1995.

As I detailed in my first book, *From Night to Light*, on Friday, January 6, 1995, a traumatic brain injury from a car accident changed my world forever. Before that day, I lived a normal, fulfilled life—worked full-time, had finished my bachelorette degree in business, and volunteered my free time to help others. After January 6, my successful work life and self-confidence suddenly became complicated and overwhelming. I couldn't understand what people were saying to me or remember the names of coworkers I had known for years. Confused and trapped inside my head, even walking and breathing seemed difficult.

My incredible journey would last 13 ½ years as I learned to function again in all areas of my life—physically, socially, cognitively, and even emotionally. Working with doctors and health-care professionals provided me the opportunity to continue to work and exist in "mainstream society." However, I didn't want to just exist—I wanted to live again!!!

I always had a strong belief in God, but after my traumatic brain injury, I soon found a deeper and more fulfilling relationship when in May of 2008 I was introduced to a personal God and His healing ability. But first I would experience new symptoms even scarier than living with the traumatic brain injury.

CHAPTER 1

New Symptoms to Battle

Just when I thought I had figured out how to cope and live with my brain injury symptoms, a new twist came into the picture on December 28, 2007. Another journey was about to begin—a journey I hadn't anticipated.

After running errands on a Friday, I arrived home to hear my phone ringing. While on the phone, I thought I saw a tiny bug flying in front of my face. I tried to follow the bug with my eyes, but it felt like my eyes were spinning inside my head. I became dizzy and disoriented but continued to talk on the phone—I really don't think there is anything that can stop me when I'm involved in a conversation. I finished my call and hung up.

I took my contacts out thinking maybe my eyes were tired and wearing my glasses instead might help. I rested the remaining part of the day and ignored what happened, thinking it to be a fluke. That night while reading, I saw a flash of light from the corner of my left eye. I recalled I had seen something similar happening earlier in the week but dismissed it as a reflection from the TV or something else. However, this time seemed different. Something weird appeared to be happening with one of my eyes. While they were open, my left eye experienced what looked like lightning bolt flashes.

The next morning, since I couldn't get an appointment to see my eye doctor, I made an appointment to see my medical doctor.

He indicated I had a floater (which appeared as a spot) in my left eye and wanted an eye doctor to check me out immediately. He recommended a local eye doctor who, after his examination, told me: "A sign of damage to the retina often produces flashes, but your retina looks fine and is intact." He gave me no other answer or explanation. At that moment, my only thought was, *You've got to be kidding.*

Okay, so here we go again with doctors, no real diagnosis, accompanied by the usual statements of "everything looks fine." However, I continued seeing flashes and now had a large black spot in the middle of my left eye. This spot didn't "float" but stayed dead center of my eye. I went home trying to handle the frequent flashes still occurring in the corner of my left eye, which also created pain, a feeling of total exhaustion, and an uneasy, unsettling feeling. Something just didn't feel right.

A couple of days later while in a store, I looked up to see something on the upper shelf. My head started spinning, and I almost blacked out and quickly grabbed hold of a cabinet. Fortunately, I didn't pass out, but everything in the room went black for what felt like an eternity. My eyes seemed to have spun into the back of my head like a character in a cartoon, and I had no clue of my surroundings. I'm sure it only lasted a few moments, but the impact dramatically affected me. I stood there for a while trying to think about what to do next—I felt dizzy, my body completely limp with no control or the ability to move. My mind immediately started to ask questions: "Will I be able to drive home? Do I have the ability to walk out of the store? What happened, and how serious is this? Should I get help?" Luckily, after a short period of time, I slowly made my way to my car and drove home, knowing something wasn't right but unable to figure out these new symptoms.

I called the doctor again. He couldn't see me but referred me to an associate who checked all my vitals and stated they were normal, but referred me to a neurologist.

Meanwhile, the flashes continued and were terrifying—they were getting worse, especially when I turned my head to the left or initiated any type of eye movement. The flashing lights became even brighter as well as painful during the evening hours when it became dark. On to yet another new journey, trying to find a neurologist.

To get an appointment took weeks while I dealt with flashes in my eyes, dizziness, disorientation, and feeling like I didn't have control of my body. At this time, I believed there was something seriously wrong with me but had no answers and no one who could help me. Meanwhile, with no answers, I had to continue to get up each day and go to work with continuing disorientation, with my body feeling weird, and knowing something wasn't working in my brain. These symptoms were scarier than when I lived with the brain injury for 13 ½ years.

The intensity in my head and eyes became so bad I headed to an urgent care facility. Anyone who knows me realizes the symptoms had to be pretty dramatic for me to seek emergency care. At the facility, I met an incredibly nice doctor who actually listened to my explanations and then took a CAT scan and my vitals. He explained my tests revealed vertigo and I would need to rest, but also wanted me to see a neurologist. I explained I had been trying to get an appointment since the first episode and had not been successful. Since I had been to the Urgent Care facility and received a diagnosis, I was then able to get an appointment in the same facility in a couple of days versus a couple of weeks.

Here we go again, I thought, *another experience meeting and working with a neurologist.* If you are familiar with my first book, *From Night to Light,* you will remember I had been to three neurologists before finally, after a ten-month period, being diagnosed with a traumatic brain injury. Each neurologist I felt didn't listen to what I had been experiencing or even appear to care about getting to the bottom of my symptoms.

Now it was twelve years into my traumatic brain injury journey, and I was back meeting with a neurologist and telling my story again. This time adding my new symptoms—all of which I had been sharing with my medical doctor, the eye doctor, and a neurologist—that I saw a bug flying in front of my face, then flashes of light and then blacked out in a store.

This new neurologist was unsympathetic and ordered more tests including an MRI and recommended seeing a neuro-ophthalmologist (an eye doctor who specializes with the brain). So off I went to another doctor to wait another couple of weeks for tests, results, and hopefully an answer. Actually, none would come. A new swirl of confusion and disappointment began with eye doctors saying the symptoms were because of the brain injury I experienced more than twelve years ago and the brain doctors indicating the symptoms were because of my eyes. No one had a real diagnosis or cure.

The days and weeks continued with no answers. The flashes increased, and the doctors now wanted me to see a retina specialist to ensure my retina had not been torn. The spot inside my left eye became bigger and looked like a big circle with a large black spot in the middle of the circle and two straight lines sticking out from the top of the circle. When I looked straight ahead it was there, and when my eyes moved it moved but never went away. It became permanent in the middle of my vision, both when my eyes were open and closed. It obscured my vision especially when working on the computer or reading anything. It proved very distracting when driving a car against the skyline, especially during cloudy days. When my eyes moved, the spot also moved causing me to be dizzy and nauseous.

Weeks and months went by, and there were still no answers. The flashes in my left eye were scary and were causing daily migraines in my eye and throughout my head. Again, no answers after having had an MRI, CAT scan, and other tests. The days were barely tolerable, but nights were worse with lightheadedness, dizziness, and disorientation. My body felt completely exhausted and unable to function correctly. I felt something was wrong with my body. When walking to the bathroom, I carried my phone, feeling at any moment I could be on the verge of passing out and absolutely no strength to even walk from room to room. Many nights I went to bed thinking I would not wake up in the morning. Before retiring to bed, I left notes around the house trying to describe my symptoms, just in case I didn't wake up in the morning. This continued for more than five months.

Then, in May of 2008, my friend Elisa invited me to a Christian ladies' conference at her church. I wasn't sure why I agreed given my symptoms and still living with the brain injury, as both made it very difficult to be out in public attending events. The session we chose was titled Mark 5:34 because it is one of my favorite Bible scriptures. I don't have a recollection of that session other than my friend leaping up from her seat totally excited about something. She knew instantly from what the speaker had shared that I could be healed of my symptoms and was determined for me to meet the speaker. You see, the session was all about healing.

The speaker shared with us that I could be completely healed of my brain injury because of Jesus's death on the cross. I'm not sure I totally understood or believed because I had seen the doctors' reports, the x-rays, and the neurological reports and they all indicated a lifelong disability. In addition, I had accepted this life of living with a brain injury. My concern and worry at that point was related to the flashes in my eye and all the other crazy symptoms I had been experiencing over the last several months.

After the May session, I started attending the church where the ladies' conference had been held. I felt a pull in my belly to go there for some reason. I perceived they had the answers on healing I had been searching for. I believed deep inside of me they could help heal me of the flashes in my eyes as well as another unrelated matter, a bone issue in my right foot that had become increasingly painful. Several years ago, I had seen a podiatrist. His diagnosis? "Stiff toe requiring surgery." In my head, after reading and meditating on the healing scriptures, I thought, *No way are they cutting into my toe or foot.* I knew Jesus could heal my foot as well as the flashes, floaters, and brain injury. As the days and weeks progressed, the foot became worse making it very difficult to walk or bend my toe. The pain became especially bad lying in bed, even with only a sheet touching my foot. The nerves in my foot and toe seemed really sensitive. Wearing shoes and walking was also a problem.

Each day I never knew what symptom I would experience and which one would behave worse—the bright lightning bolt-like flash in my eye, the big black spot impacting my vision, the limp and pain in my right foot, or the brain injury symptoms I had lived with for more than 13 ½ years.

One Sunday in July 2008, as I hobbled into church wearing sneakers, I shared with Elisa my difficultly in walking and the increase of the flashes in my eye, including some other new symptoms. For months I had been dealing with all of these symptoms alone. I didn't share with anyone as I thought people would think I was either crazy or a chronic complainer. Even I couldn't believe all these symptoms were impacting my life all at the same time.

After service, Elisa brought me to see Cathy, one of the worship leaders, who had shared the healing scriptures with me at the conference in May. I felt like I was babbling when I met with her as there were so many things happening to me and I didn't know where to begin or how anyone could possibly help me. She prayed over me and told me to walk on my foot—and as I put my foot down, I walked without the limp and without pain. Amazing! I believed what she prayed and spoke over me and knew I was healed. Could it be that simple? The toe didn't bend yet, but she told me to continue to stand firm in God's Word and keep speaking healing over my foot and body. This became daily and, at times, an hourly conversation with myself. I needed to continue to renew my mind to the fact I was healed by God's grace and glory. Romans 12:2 says, *And do not be conformed to this world, but be transformed by the renewing of your mind, so that you may prove what the will of God is, that which is good and acceptable and perfect* (NASB).

During these years, my body felt like it was under attack. When attending church, I would meet Cathy, and she shared healing scriptures with me like Isaiah 53:5 [*But He was wounded for our transgressions, He was bruised for our iniquities; The chastisement for our peace was upon Him, And by His stripes we are healed* (NKJV)]. Other healing scriptures were shared each Sunday at church service. I wrote every one down and even looked up new ones so I could read, meditate, and completely fill my mind with what God's Word said about healing. I also listened to a tape Cathy provided me and devoured different Christian websites that taught about healing. I became obsessed with what God revealed about His healing touch. I believed in the same miracles in the Bible and the flashes and other medical symptoms had to disappear. (My focus wasn't on the brain injury at this time because of the intensity of the other symptoms.) Many times the messages I read and heard were "walk by faith." I thought seriously, *What does that really mean? How does one do that?*

In my own way of thinking to demonstrate the principle of "walking by faith," I decided to remove a green bracelet I wore designed to raise awareness about brain injuries. I also decided to park my car at work in the main parking area behind our office building where everyone else parked their cars, instead of the handicapped space directly in front of the building. This presented a long walk for me as well as an uphill incline at the end of the day which would challenge my body and brain. Previously, for some reason, my body couldn't physically handle walking up an incline, and it caused a lot of pain inside my head. In addition, with hundreds of cars parked in the same lot, my brain couldn't focus or recall where I had parked my car. Nevertheless, in order to "walk by faith," I needed to completely believe and stand on my faith that I had been healed of the brain injury (even though I still experienced all the symptoms) and demonstrate it. Therefore, I removed the "handicap" sticker and parked my car in the large lot behind my office building. The next Sunday after removing my green bracelet and the "handicap" parking sticker from my car, my life dramatically changed again!

At the end of the church service, one of our worship leaders who had been preaching asked anyone who needed healing to come up to the altar. I chose not to go to the altar as in my mind I believed God's promises and that I had been healed, though I still lived with all my dramatic symptoms. I felt if I went up for prayer, it would show I doubted Jesus had already healed me. I wanted to do everything correctly and not miss out on my healing. A few minutes later, the worship leader asked everyone at the altar to take a step back, and he called others to the altar. I don't have any recollection about what he said, but my friend Elisa heard the call and literally pulled me with her to the altar. She heard the worship leader ask anyone to come forward who believed for a manifestation of their healing—someone waiting for what they were believing would become visible. God had spoken to Elisa to get me to the altar, and she obeyed quickly. I don't think my feet even touched the floor. I was like a cartoon character where someone has you by the hand and your feet are up in the air flapping in the wind similar to a kite. Within seconds and without realizing, I was standing at the front of the church, and my body violently shaking.

The worship leader placed his hands on my head, and the shaking stopped instantly. I'm not sure I really understood what happened, for it wasn't completely revealed to me until my drive home from church. While at the altar, Elisa had her hand on my back and could feel the shaking in my body. She then felt it dramatically stop, and at that exact moment she shared a vision with me as we walked back to our seats. In her mind she saw an egg timer go ding—it hit zero! We both didn't know what it meant and thought it's strange, but she felt it signaled something had stopped, meaning something was over. With all the strange things happening to me, I really couldn't process an egg timer going ding. ☺ However, Jesus knew exactly what that meant, and He revealed it to me while driving home.

In my car, Jesus opened my eyes and gave me understanding about the scriptures I had been reading and meditating on—similar to what He did for the two disciples on the road to Emmaus three days after Jesus's death. At that moment in the car, I knew I had been healed of the brain injury—I knew that I knew that I knew! There wasn't a doubt in my mind. It felt like something just lifted from my head and floated away. The pain in my head from the brain injury I lived with 24/7 for 13 ½ years completely vanished in an instant. When you have lived with the type of pain I had for so many years, you know instantly when something is different. I even noticed my mind and entire brain felt awake for the first time in many, many years. Amen, Amen, Amen! God is so amazing, awesome, and incredible!

Now completely alert, I remember saying to God that I didn't need any proof or doctors telling me I had been healed. I knew without a shadow of doubt my God, the great Physician, my Healer, had completely restored my brain. Even though I didn't need proof, our God is so good that over the next couple of days He started to reveal to me and provide proof of my complete healing. I believe this was to show those around me the proof of my healing.

Soon after this instant miracle, we were having a bridal shower at the office for one of my coworkers. Each of us in attendance received a bridal shower game to complete. The first game required us to match as many celebrity couples on a sheet of paper. For example, we received the name Lucille Ball and needed to answer with Desi Arnaz. At first, I panicked; being a very competitive person, I didn't like to lose at anything. These types of situations are very challenging for a brain injury survivor. You aren't able to think quickly, and with others in the room talking, it made it even harder to process the instructions and try to come up with the answers. But then I quickly remembered my brain had been completely healed, and I started to look at the names on the list, and the answers came popping into my head—I knew almost every answer. Out of the twenty questions, I missed only two. Interesting and how exciting! Not only had I been the first one to finish, but I blew away the competition of my coworkers. The next person wasn't even close to the number I had answered correctly. Amazing how much God cares for us. He not only began to show me how completely healed I was but also provided opportunities to demonstrate my healing so others could fully understand the extent of my healing. We played another game at the bridal shower, and again I won. This was getting funny and at the same time incredible. Later in the week, I received copies of my brain scan the neuro-ophthalmologist had taken for the flashes in my eyes—another miracle! The brain scan also showed no damage to my brain. To this doctor, there weren't any signs of the former brain injury. The doctor mentioned that someone who had a brain injury over 13 years ago should have shown deterioration over the years, but mine showed nothing. Amen—praise God! It was another illustration from God showing my complete healing, even though I knew it that moment in the car. God showed me and others His awesome healing grace. In the days and months ahead, others would need proof of my healing, and God surely delivered it. I used these examples to show others the awesome miracle of how at one moment in time I had an injured and damaged brain and in an instant was totally healed.

My journey took a new twist as I learned to live without a brain injury and while still living with my eye issues. For some reason, I never told anyone of the healing as I don't think I really understood the magnitude of what happened that day in the car. How could I explain it? How was I going to live now without a brain injury after all these years? I was overwhelmed and I think a little scared by this realization and chose to keep it quietly to myself—in addition, I still had other symptoms, like the flashes, the floaters, and the bone issue. I struggled to understand how my brain could be healed but the other symptoms were still around. However, God had other ideas.

During a Sunday school class, healing was the discussion topic. I remember raising my hand and mentioning I had been healed from a brain injury after 13 ½ years. This is very uncharacteristic for me. I have now come to realize when God wants me to share something, I end up raising my hand and speaking out loud without realizing I'm doing it. It kind of just happens. I'm also learning when God wants me to share something, it is Him speaking through me.

Shortly after sharing my story in the Sunday school class, I received a call from one of the elders at my friend's church—the one I was now attending regularly. The elder asked me to share my testimony at the Thanksgiving Eve service. I thought, *Wow, really? Seriously, me?* What did I have to share? I thought a testimony was how you came to know Jesus as your Savior. I didn't realize my testimony was going to be about how God healed me. I sheepishly agreed to speak and then realized this was going to be the first time I would speak about how God healed my brain. The Thanksgiving Eve service was beautiful, and the testimonies were amazing. I thought, *Wow, I don't really have much to share*, as others shared about being healed of cancer and tumors. The agenda listed me as the last to speak, and my nerves continued to grow. At the service, my friend Elisa, who is never far from my side, told me to just speak from my heart. When I do this, I feel God enables me to share what He believes others need to hear. This continues to be the best advice. As I started to speak, my nerves vanished, and I know my thoughts and words were given to me by the Holy Spirit. I shared the awesome journey that God enabled me to experience—it felt like the words just flowed out of my mouth. At that time, I didn't realize how many lives were touched, but found out later how many people remembered my testimony and shared it with others and also how it impacted so many and drew them closer to God.

After realizing what an incredible miracle I lived through, I started sharing my testimony with everyone I met. At times it was challenging to speak about God's healing of my brain while I still struggled with my eyes and foot. About a month after sharing my testimony, I started to experience flashes and floaters in my right eye. So now, throughout the day and night, both eyes were flashing—sometimes up to a hundred times a day.

I realized I was in a battle, but I was not about to doubt the incredible healing that God shared with me. I knew one day the manifestation of the healing of my eyes and foot would happen.

But, how long would I have to wait?

CHAPTER 2

Listening for That Still Small Voice

I stood firm in my belief that my eyes were healed and patiently waited for the manifestation of my miracle. While sitting on my sofa on January 5, 2009, I heard what sounded like a small voice coming from my belly saying, "It is done; it is over." I leaped from the sofa and ran to the mirror believing God was letting me know the lightning bolt flashes and floaters were gone and I was healed. I looked in the mirror but forgot the flashes and floaters were inside my eyes and not visible to the naked eye. For a moment I questioned God but never doubted His promise.

When I continued to see the flashes and floaters in the coming days, I had a feeling of disappointment but continued to believe I heard from God. I stood firm on His promise—"It is done; it is over." Amazingly, the January 5 date was one day before the anniversary date (January 6) of my car accident that dramatically changed the course of my life and began my incredible journey with God. I remember thinking how awesome God spoke to me on the eve of my fourteenth year anniversary of the accident.

As the months progressed and I kept hearing messages on being healed and to "stand firm," I wanted to better understand the whole experiences concerning my eyes, body, and foot. I spent time reading the healing scriptures in my Bible and meditated as much as possible. Because of the flashes and floaters in my eyes, at times it made it difficult to read my Bible with the spots swirling right in front of my vision causing distraction and pain in my eyes and head. Many times it made me nauseous; nevertheless, my focus and goal remained the same—to grow deeper in my faith journey. I went to church every Sunday and started attending Sunday school classes before service and even registered for Bible college which enabled me to take classes at night. I felt like a sponge, wanting to absorb as much as possible. Each week I experienced new and strange symptoms in my body and brain, but I continued to press into God and wait patiently for the day when all my symptoms would disappear.

My journey with God, as you'll see, continued daily, becoming more incredible and awesome with each passing day, week, and month. During the times I struggled in my healing journey, I recalled that still small voice I heard on January 5, and it kept me standing firm in my belief for the manifestation of my healing. I knew my symptoms were only moments away from leaving my body for good. This made me determined to experience life, now after being grounded for 13 ½ years. It was time to set sail.

Setting Sail

On June 18, 2009, the day began with pouring rain but with great expectations of a new and exciting experience in my life which included an Alaskan cruise which had been one of my dreams and goals in life—something I never felt I'd accomplish after sustaining my brain injury.

The roads to the airport were incredibly dangerous as I prepared for my long plane ride to Seattle, Washington, to board a ship for my Alaska adventure, and here we were just twenty-four hours away. I knew deep down my destiny included being on this trip. How did I know this? Something began happening five months earlier when I first thought about my next vacation and realized I had not been on a vacation for almost two years because of health issues. Stressed from work and needing to spend quiet time away with God to restore my energy, my daily prayer time included asking what to do for a vacation. My answer came in a couple of days when I received an e-mail about a Christian singles cruise in June to Alaska. At first I thought, *I don't take June vacations,* so I ignored the e-mail. Then while working with my physical therapist, he asked me my vacation plans, suggesting I needed some time away. I shared with him the e-mail about the cruise, and he immediately suggested I go. I also mentioned the idea to some friends in the hopes someone could accompany me, but no one was able to get away during the time of the cruise.

Funny how at times different thoughts pop into our heads—and even funnier was this thought that surfaced in my mind, *If God really wants me to go on this cruise, then the Royal Caribbean cruise line will call me.* I remember chuckling at the thought. When I mentioned this jokingly to my friends, they laughed along with me at the impossibility of the Royal Caribbean cruise line actually calling me personally.

That night when I got home from work, I received a voice message on my phone from someone at Royal Caribbean cruise line asking if they could help me book a trip. My initial reaction was what a strange message and quickly dismissed it. Days later I recalled my phone message and mentioned it to a friend, and she thought it had to be a sign. She reminded me of the thought I had about if God wanted me to go on this cruise, Royal Caribbean would call me.

So now my attention and focus went back to the e-mail I had received about the Alaskan cruise. I prayed again and asked God, "If you really want me to go on this trip, let me know." Again upon returning home from work, I received the same message on my answering machine from the Royal Caribbean cruise line asking if they could help me book a cruise. Amazingly, I dismissed it again, not connecting the dots between my questions to God about whether I should go. I know many of you reading this are saying, "How can she be missing these signs?" But, in my own way of thinking and processing, I expected to hear directly from God with a yes or no answer to my specific question if I should go on this June Christian singles cruise. "Could these phone messages have been orchestrated by God?" I continued to pray and ask God about this as my attention and questions now turned to the cost of this trip. Since I would be traveling alone, the cost of the cabin doubled in price; however, with the group rate, it seemed to be reasonable compared to what I had paid on past cruises. My hesitation related to being a good steward of God's money. My prayers to God now included asking Him if I should spend all this money on a vacation when we were experiencing a recession in our country and many of my friends and others around me were struggling with money issues and finances.

That Sunday, while watching Dr. Charles Stanley (a Christian minister) on TV, he read an e-mail from someone with the exact same question I raised to God. Dr. Stanley replied, "Yes, you should take a vacation if you can afford it," indicating "If you could afford it, you would also be helping to stimulate the economy." I couldn't believe it was the exact question I asked God about, but in my mind I thought I needed to hear directly from God. I'm not sure what I had expected—maybe actually hearing God's voice answering yes or no at the exact moment I asked my question.

Again, I prayed, adding an additional question, "Should I go alone because my friends couldn't go?" Typically, I had never gone on a vacation alone. I always went with friends. Right after asking this question, I happened to be watching Joyce Meyer (another Christian teacher on TV). She made a statement about how important it is to go on vacation alone, to spend time with God. I thought, *Wow, all the questions I had asked God have been answered.* I started to realize maybe God uses other people to address and answer our questions to Him. I know you are now all saying, "How come you didn't connect the dots sooner?" As you can see in this situation, I truly didn't connect the dots, not realizing how God communicates with us. And, I'm sure, each time I asked another question, I can only imagine God with His head in His hands saying something like "Why aren't you getting this?" along with a smile and chuckle. I now faced my last hurdle. The trip was scheduled to leave on a Sunday and return on a Sunday and was booked with a cruise line other than Royal Caribbean. I was feeling uncomfortable traveling on the Lord's day, as I didn't want to miss two Sundays at my church.

So here we go again. I went to God and asked Him about traveling on Sunday and letting Him know I typically only cruised on the Royal Caribbean line. Over the weekend, I received an e-mail about a Christian cruise to Alaska traveling from Friday to Friday on the Royal Caribbean. I thought, *Wow, now every one of my questions and concerns have been answered.* Even the cost of this trip was cheaper.

I became excited at the possibility of this cruise and on Monday morning called the travel agent and inquired about the trip details. It turned out to be the exact same trip I had been praying about—the one leaving from Sunday to Sunday. The travel agent moved the entire trip to the Royal Caribbean cruise line because of a better rate.

I signed up immediately having finally connected the dots and realizing God wanted me on this particular cruise. I shared my story with the travel agent, describing how many times God answered my questions about this trip but I hadn't been listening or connecting the dots. She was thrilled to know God was truly involved with my trip. Her team had been praying about this trip to Alaska, and she felt my story helped validate her prayers. I signed up in February for the June cruise and knew without a shadow of a doubt I was supposed to be on that ship sailing to Alaska. However, something else began happening.

During the months and weeks leading up to the trip, the medical symptoms I had been living with for the last months and years were now increasing and becoming more intense. My thoughts turned immediately to *What if I can't make the trip to Alaska? What if my symptoms got worse?* I quickly realized the negative thoughts trying to creep into my mind, and I immediately dismissed them and continued saying, "I know I'm supposed to be on this cruise!"

Two weeks before the sail date, the flashes became really intense causing severe migraines in my eyes. At the same time, the bone alignment in my right toe became even more painful making it difficult to walk. For years now I only wore flat shoes and wondered, *How am I going to wear a fancy cocktail dress on the cruise with flat plain shoes?* My focus quickly turned to God. I knew He would enable me to wear fancy high-heeled shoes with a beautiful dress on the night of the captain's dinner.

Struggling with my symptoms, I continued to stand firm in God's promise of healing. The battlefield was in my mind, and it was important for me not to get discouraged by the symptoms I felt. But how could I not when my symptoms dealt with walking and seeing? These are important body parts designed to get one through each day.

Then, on May 31 (two weeks before the sail date), I awoke feeling something was going to happen today. I had no idea what this meant. It was just a feeling something big was about to happen. I went about my normal day and attended Sunday school class and the worship service. I felt God's presence so strong. I had heightened expectations that maybe this could be the day of the manifestation of all my symptoms—the day the spots in my eyes and the flashes would vanish and the bone in my foot align correctly to eliminate my daily pain.

In the middle of worship, many were making their way to the altar, including my friend Elisa who grabbed my arm and pulled me along with her, again! As I reached the altar, tears were streaming down my face. I'm not sure why, except many times when God showed up tears usually occurred. There were others at the altar, and I expected the pastor planned to lay hands on everyone and pray for them. My mind raced. "Wow, this must be it—this is the feeling I had this morning. I'm going to experience the manifestation." I felt my spirit getting excited and my heart began to beat faster. After only a few moments, everyone started to return to their seats, and the service started.

My first thought was *Did I miss something?* Then I quickly thought, *Okay, maybe I'm going to hear a word during the sermon, and my expected feeling will happen during the service.* I could feel God's presence, and I patiently waited for my special moment.

The service concluded, and as we started to walk out, the pastor's wife stopped to speak with me. "How are you doing, Donna? I'd like to share that I can truly see God's glory in you." Those few words were about to change my life. I felt finally validated after the enemy had been speaking lies into my life for so many years. I really did have God in my life. Now I had learned how to stop the lies and listen more closely to what God's Word said. My friend Elisa was never far from my side and shared with the pastor's wife my continuing struggle with so many health issues that, at times, often paralyzed me.

She said, "Maybe you could spend some time with me so I can help you handle these symptoms while you wait patiently for them to disappear." She said she'd be happy to speak with me but wanted to pray for me before I left church. My pastor's wife referenced James 5:14–15, *Are any of you sick? You should call for the elders of the church to come and pray over you, anointing you with oil in the name of the Lord. Such a prayer offered in faith will heal the sick, and the Lord will make you well* (NLT). She went to the altar to get anointing oil and then seemed to disappear. We waited for what seemed like an endless amount of time, while I grew uncomfortable and uneasy. I never liked sharing my struggles with others, preferring to handle my issues in private and not have others know what's wrong with me.

When she returned, she brought the pastor with her. My initial thought? *Oh boy, they are bringing out the big guns for me—I must really be in bad shape.* At this point, I was even more uncomfortable as I felt all the attention on me and preferred blending into the background. The pastor prayed for my eyes and toe and then placed his hand on my left shoulder and told me I needed to believe and accept the healing message and to give thanks to Jesus. His words were soft and comforting, like a father speaking to a daughter. What a powerful experience for me as the pastor simulated God speaking to me. What a day! I finally felt like one of God's children and, even more importantly, felt like God's daughter. I left church knowing my life was going to be different. Amazingly, the next day, Elisa told me the pastor's wife never told him about my eyes or my toe. God had spoken to him while in his office and told him he needed to pray with me.

At work I started crying, overwhelmed with emotion about how much God loved me and realizing He spoke directly to the pastor to pray for me about my eyes and toe. I knew waking up that day something special was going to happen to me, and it did—I found a deeper and closer relationship with Father God. This was only the beginning of greater experiences to come in the days and weeks ahead.

Excited for my cruise, I continued to stand firm in God's Word and in the messages and prayers that had been spoken over me. God used my pastor and his wife to give me the confidence to travel and walk by faith through whatever pain or symptoms that might arise. This would be the first time traveling alone without a friend or someone I knew alongside me since living with my traumatic brain injury in 1995.

How would I do?

CHAPTER 3

A Trip of a Lifetime

On June 17, 2009, one day away from my Alaskan cruise, I wanted to be in the house of the Lord. I decided to attend a morning healing class at church. I had been preparing to go since the beginning of the week. I set out to drive the twenty minutes to the class and got stuck in bumper-to-bumper traffic. I started to panic realizing I would be late for class, which wasn't acceptable as I don't like being late for anything. Negative thoughts raced through my mind: "You are going to be embarrassed showing up late for class and walking in after everyone is seated. They'll stare at you." By now, I started getting wise to negative comments flitting in my head, so I countered immediately and said, "No way. God is going to open up this traffic just like He parted the Red Sea for the Israelites!" I calmly sat in traffic expecting something to happen when all of a sudden the road opened up and I continued on my way. See, I knew God wanted me to attend this healing class. My instincts told me the class wouldn't begin until I arrived, and it turned out I was only five minutes late and the class began the moment I arrived. I smiled knowing God had absolutely perfect timing. After the class, I had an opportunity to speak with my friend Cathy who teaches the healing class and who had been my mentor on healing after meeting her in May 2008 at the women's conference. I told her my Alaska vacation began tomorrow and how

God told me several times to go on this cruise, and I knew there was something special about to happen. She agreed.

I left the class and headed for Kessler Institute to complete a questionnaire which helped the brain injury organization provide better service for survivors. As I waited in the lobby, I met one of the women who also had a brain injury. (I had helped her many years ago when she was first diagnosed.) I shared with her I was leaving the next day on a Christian cruise. She mentioned she was also a Christian, and I shared my testimony on how God healed my brain. I also provided scriptures on healing, telling her healing was available to her as well because God is not a respecter of persons. Romans 2:11 shows us *For God does not show favoritism* (NLT). I told her as soon as I got home I would send her the healing scriptures I meditated on each day. What an exciting and humbling experience to be able to share how God still provides miracles today.

While working on the questionnaire with the Kessler research assistant, I again shared my testimony on how God healed my brain and I no longer had to live with the effects of the brain injury. As I left Kessler that afternoon, it was a bright beautiful sunny day. I happened to look up at the blue sky and white puffy clouds and thankfully expressed to God, "How incredible! In a span of an hour, I was able to share my testimony twice." At that moment I heard the words, "Tell all the world. Tell all the world," and it felt like the words were coming from the sky and through those beautiful white cumulous clouds. What an awesome moment. I sat in my car amazed by the experience and thought, *Seriously, how am I going to tell the whole world?*

The next morning I got up early and headed to the airport to begin my Alaska journey. The weather was bad as it had been raining for hours, and the roads were slippery. I calmly sat in the back seat of the car service and knew everything would be alright. At the airport I made it through ticketing and airport security easily, no lines, no hassles. Before going to my gate, I met up with a woman, Leah, from my home state traveling on the same trip. The travel agent had connected us before the trip. We instantly became friends and made arrangements to meet at the coffee shop at the airport. How exciting to meet someone new and now be on the journey with someone and no longer traveling solo. Unfortunately, we didn't sit together on the plane, but we boarded together and caught up once the plane landed.

As you can imagine with all my challenges and a six-hour flight ahead of me, it left me with anxious feelings. A previous four-hour flight a couple of years earlier caused weird symptoms and pain in my legs and body. So you can envision my thoughts about what could happen on a six-hour trip. However, I knew God would be with me on this trip. I had enough mileage points to upgrade my seat to first class providing me more leg room and accommodations should I start feeling any symptoms. I'm sure God made these arrangements for me to sit next to a nice Christian woman. She told me she had been a Christian for a long time, and I felt blessed to be able to spend this time listening to her and learning even more about the God I loved. She and her friends were running a marathon in Seattle to raise awareness and money for a charity. It was a perfect opening for me to then share my testimony on how I lived with the brain injury and about my healing and yet another opportunity within days God had given me to share His healing grace. We chatted for a while and then spent some alone time with God while way up in the sky. Amazing how close you can feel to God while on an airplane.

We arrived in Seattle around lunchtime. The hotel provided a service to take us to the hotel where we spent the night and met up with other Christian singles for our Alaska adventure. My new friend, Leah, had a Christian high school friend living in Seattle, and they both invited me to spend the afternoon with them. In the past, I would have begged out of the invite not only so I wouldn't tire myself out but also because I didn't know the lay of the land and any potential challenges. However, this time, it was a new me and a new adventure!

We had a great lunch together. What a wonderful experience to spend time with new friends, sharing our stories about how God impacted our lives. After lunch, we were given a tour of Seattle. First stop of course was the Space Needle and going up in the elevator. I could hear the voice in my head screaming, "You can't do that. It is too high up. What if you get dizzy in the elevator? What if you have a panic attack? How embarrassing that will be in front of your new friends!"

I immediately squashed those negative thoughts, knowing with God all things were possible and together we could overcome any fear and doubt and make it to the top of the Space Needle. I got into the jam-packed elevator. I became overwhelmed with excitement to do something I hadn't done in more than thirteen years. Years ago it would have been impossible to be crammed into an elevator with other people.

I felt the elevator slowly stop and the doors open and then heard in my head, *We did it!!!* The elevator door opened, and what my eyes saw first was a shirt with "I made it to the top of the Space Needle." I knew this was a message for me and I had to buy it. Two emotions flooded through me—the excitement of overcoming my first challenge of this trip and the feeling of being on top of the world. I hadn't been able to do something like this in a very long time because of the brain injury and its symptoms. I stood firm and walked by faith over five hundred feet above the earth. The Space Needle is an observation tower in Seattle, Washington, with a rotating restaurant standing at five hundred feet. With the rotating restaurant and the height of the Space Needle, you can imagine this was an amazing achievement.

Evening approached, and I said goodbye to Leah's high school friend and headed to the hotel to unwind. The time difference started to kick in (I had flown from the east coast to the west coast). While getting ready for bed, I removed my contacts and put on my glasses, something I've been doing most of my life. As I put the glasses on, the tip of the arm poked right through the inside corner of my left eye. It felt like it went right through to the back of my eye. For a moment I sat stunned, wondering if my eye still worked. After composing myself, I realized there didn't appear to be any damage to my eye. How could that be when the poke was pretty intense and went straight into the corner of my eye? But my eye was fine; I could see perfectly and there was no pain. "What just happened? How did I poke myself and not lose my eye completely?" It is amazing how quickly panic can set in and your mind race to negative thoughts like seeing yourself being rushed to the hospital and missing the ship departing the next day. I went to sleep dismissing what happened, nevertheless a little anxious waiting for morning and my journey to begin.

Leah and I met up for breakfast. Later, in the hotel lobby, we met everyone else going on the cruise. At first glance, everyone seemed really nice and excited to begin our Alaska adventure. We boarded a bus to take us to the ship. Upon arriving at the ship, we unloaded our luggage, during which time the trip leader approached me and mentioned I had a beautiful smile and saw the glory of the Lord shining through me. It was almost the same comment expressed by my pastor's wife two weeks earlier, and that simple comment from the leader gave me the courage and confidence for the rest of the trip. I typically lack confidence when meeting new people and have a tendency to be shy and quiet. I believe God used her to provide me with the confirmation I needed to show me others saw me as a child of God, something I had struggled with for a very long time.

We boarded the ship, unpacked our luggage, and then went to meet with the other trip members. There were a total of twenty-five of us, twenty-two women and three men. We felt sorry for the guys, but they turned out to be real troopers putting up with all of us women. The majority of the time, the twenty-five of us remained together. We all had dinner together each night and participated in praise and worship services throughout the week—an awesome time of fellowshipping and meeting other Christian singles.

The first night the seas inside the Alaska strait were very rough. The captain warned us, but as a seasoned cruiser, having been on many ships and boats before, I really didn't pay much attention. Many years ago I had been on a ship traveling in front of a hurricane and never got seasick, so I didn't really expect any issues. Returning to my cabin to get ready for bed, I felt the rocking of the ship and expected the rocking motion to help me sleep. Just before getting into bed, my nose started bleeding. The flow was extremely heavy. I don't ever recall having a bloody nose and especially not to this degree. I laid flat and tilted my head back to try and stop the bleeding. This was incredible, first poking myself in my eye and now a bloody nose. What was happening? I felt dizzy. I thought it might be because I had lost a lot of blood, but then I happened to look down and saw my left foot was black and blue. The entire toe area and top of my foot looked the deepest black and blue I had ever seen. I sat there amazed and in shock. What could this be? How did this happen? My only thought was I wanted to get off the ship and wondered how quickly we would be reaching the first port so I could fly home. The dizziness increased, and I didn't feel well. I couldn't explain what happened the night before when the stem of my glasses poked my eye and couldn't explain the bloody nose and now my black and blue foot. The only thing to do was try to sleep. Luckily, I fell asleep easily and woke up to extremely rocky seas.

Having put the strange happenings of the night before behind me, I got ready for breakfast and meeting up with our group for morning worship. While in my tiny bathroom, I started feeling weird. Never having been hit with seasickness, I had no idea what was wrong. In addition, over the years, I always seemed to be experiencing weird things—but this was a new, strange feeling. I attempted a shower and soon realized I might have seasickness. I did get sick to my stomach once, but determined to dress and meet the others. This was not about to stop me. Besides, I needed to get out of the cabin room. I knew staying in the cabin would make me feel worse.

I met a couple of the ladies from our traveling group for breakfast but couldn't put anything in my stomach. I tried a bagel and took only a couple of nibbles. To explain why I wasn't eating breakfast, I shared with my new traveling friend, Leah, I had gotten seasick. As we headed to our morning meeting, I carried with me a napkin and some water. I thought at least I could be prepared in case I got sick. As a true planner, I always anticipate all possibilities for any given situation. I know, my poor brain, it is always working overtime.

At our first conference session together, we learned half the group was in bed sick. The other half seemed to be fine at weathering the stormy sea. The remaining group shared they were either wearing seasickness patches or had taken something. I had never taken anything and at this point didn't want to put anything in my stomach. I can be pretty determined when I need to be, and I chose to fight through the symptoms.

Our first group activity turned out to be a scavenger hunt around the ship. I thought, *Oh boy, this is going to be fun.* We were teamed up with three other members and had to read a clue (scripture in the Bible) and then determine the answer from the scripture. Once we had the answers to each of the scripture clues, we had to run around the ship taking a picture of the answer. Being a competitive person, I believe it helped me overcome my seasickness since my entire focus was on winning this game. I completely forgot about any ailments I was feeling. As we raced around the ship snapping pictures of items and having a great time, my seasickness symptoms left. The extra bonus was getting to know my teammates and new friends.

Of course, we were the first team back to home base which counted as additional points. We handed over our captured pictures to the trip leaders. As the others returned from their hunt, everyone seemed to be mingling and having a great time—well, at least the ones who were upright and still standing. The other half of our group was still in bed dealing with seasickness. I can honestly say I believe our team won the overall competition. The entire group needed to review everyone's pictures and answers; and, upon doing so, everyone's competitive nature surfaced, and they started disqualifying our answers. It got pretty ugly at times. ☺ In the end I think we came in second, and the winning team won gift certificates to Starbucks. Since I'm not a coffee drinker, it made losing a little easier, but as I'm writing this I know in my heart we were really the winners. I don't sound like a competitive person, do I?

Our afternoon session took us to the top of the ship where we talked about our lives and experiences living as single Christians. I sat quietly which is typical for me when I'm around new people especially in a group setting. In addition, I think I needed to find my sea legs. Before the session even began, our assigned pastor, Pastor Joel, asked how everyone was feeling and if anyone was seasick. He mentioned his wife hadn't been able to get out of bed yet. Leah shared with Pastor Joel that I didn't feel well, which would not have been anything I volunteered publicly. He asked how I was doing, and I told him I was fine, just a little trouble in the morning. Throughout the next hour or two, the group talked and shared comments, while I had the feeling the pastor was watching me. Could it have been because I hadn't felt well or because I had been the only person who didn't have anything to say or add? Hmm, not sure. But at the end of the session, he approached me and asked if I was okay. I reassured him I was fine and shared with him my eye issues for the last year which I thought could have caused my seasickness. His curious nature kicked in and inquired about my eyes, so I shared about the floaters and flashes and stated I was healed because I had previously been healed of a brain injury and knew about God's healing ability. I think we sat and spoke for almost an hour. He was completely amazed at my story and congratulated me on my bravery for traveling for so many miles while I still had issues with my eyes. I told him I knew God wanted me on this trip and shared how I got here.

I was glad the conversation I had was just between me and the pastor. My goal for this trip was not to be the brain injury survivor. I wanted to find out who I was as a whole, healed person since I felt like I had lost "me" for those many years. I needed to find the new "me."

At dinner I sat next to Leah and one of the guys from our scavenger hunt, and we laughed the entire night. Everyone seemed to instantly connect with each other. We swapped stories about how God had been working in our lives. I ate my dinner, and the memory of the seasickness was a distant memory.

The next day was Sunday, and we were all up early and ready to worship together. There is something awesome and special about worshipping with other believers out in the middle of the ocean. Toward the end of the service, Pastor Joel stopped and asked our permission to end a little early as he wanted to share an amazing story he heard the day before. We were all interested, and I looked around to see if I could figure out whom he would pick. Over the course of our first two days, I had heard some amazing stories from the others. All of a sudden I heard him call my name and ask if I would feel comfortable sharing my story. I remember being in shock and sitting there staring at him for a few moments when I realized everyone was now staring at me. My initial thought was *How could my story be amazing when there were so many others who have lived through incredible journeys?*

I hesitantly got up from my seat and headed to the front of the room. This would now be my second time in only a few short months to tell my story about being healed. I had spoken many times about living with a brain injury; however, my story now centered on my healing. I could feel everyone's eyes focused on me as I had been very quiet the first day and a half, and I'm sure they were wondering if I even had a voice.

I spoke about the accident and the symptoms, and the room was completely silent. I watched my shipmates sitting on the edge of their seats so as not to miss any of my story. The door to our room had been open, and in the corner of my eye I could see other passengers standing in the doorway also listening. Sometimes it feels like you are outside of your body. You know you are standing there speaking, and at the same time you feel like you are watching yourself from a distance because it just couldn't be you in front of people speaking. I know God had to be there in that moment because after I finished speaking, I couldn't recall all what I had shared. My shipmates told me later how much God spoke to their hearts through my story.

After finishing speaking, and before I sat down, Pastor Joel asked me to stay so he and the others could pray for me since I had mentioned the symptoms I continued to experience. As the pastor prayed, he suddenly stopped and paused. The pause felt like forever as I conspicuously stood up in front of everyone and felt quite self-conscious. Pastor Joel shared the insight God gave him: "Thousands will hear her story." I didn't know what to think about this revelation. I continued to be amazed at how much God moves in my life and speaks to others about me. In these kinds of moments, I feel God as a Father protecting and watching out for His daughter.

For the rest of the day and throughout the trip, my shipmates approached me to share how my story impacted and touched their lives. One woman had lost her husband to an illness. She mentioned they had been believing and praying for his healing, and after his death she stopped believing. She told me how uncomfortable she felt when she arrived on the ship, feeling she didn't belong. "After hearing your testimony," she said, "I knew exactly why I was on this trip. The money I spent was worth the entire trip just to hear your story." I was humbled to think God could use me to help this woman and realized why God wanted me on this trip. He wanted me to share my story.

Another woman conveyed to me: "I've been asking God to show me a miracle like in the Old Testament days. I believe God answered my prayer through your story." Again, I was humbled and overwhelmed with emotions by her words. How incredible God is to use each of us. These stories continued throughout the ten days on the ship. Each person in our little group had been touched by my testimony of what God had done in my life.

The beauty of Alaska, the incredible views, and God's awesome mountains, along with the quality time spent with new friends, were life changing. My body and brain were healthy enough to travel. I got to ride on a dog sled, saw numerous whales during an excursion, received a personal tour of the captain's bridge, and wore my fancy high-heeled shoes without pain in my toe and foot. I even learned how to dance a little—something I hadn't been able to do since the brain injury. My ten-day Alaska trip turned out to be an incredible and awesome experience. How blessed can one person be?

On the plane ride home, reflecting back on all the incredible experiences, I felt I might not have spent enough time with God to quietly meditate on His Word. This had been one of my initial goals and the reason I had ventured on this trip alone—to spend time alone on the deck, look out into the ocean, and listen for God to speak to my heart with guidance and instruction on what is next for my life. I started to feel bad realizing I might have missed God's message.

As the plane taxied from the terminal, I pulled out my Bible and started reading and thanking God for this incredible trip. As I prayed and meditated, I could hear God say to me, "You always wanted to be a nurse and help people; but you are going to help and heal people in a different way." My heart felt so full of love and thrilled to think God wanted to use my experiences to help others. I couldn't wait to get home to share my incredible ten-day journey with my friends. I anticipated great months of clear sailing ahead.

Or so I thought.

CHAPTER 4

Ready to Give Up

I had no idea my health issues were about to take a turn for the worse. Although I had been completely healed of the brain injury, my struggle with the lightning bolt flashes in my eyes grew more intense. Not only did they make my nights challenging and scary, but in the spring of 2009 I registered for Bible college and attended my first official class called "Song of the Lord," and the flashes in my eyes made attention and focus in class difficult. I not only grappled with that, but a new condition developed that terrified me.

But before I relate what that new problem was, let me back up and mention some non-health problems I also encountered.

One particular class turned into a night of praising God with everyone on their feet and hands raised in the air in complete worship to our Lord. This style of praising God was new for me, and I became uncomfortable. My thoughts swirled with a feeling of not belonging. Comments bombarded my mind such as *You aren't really a Christian. You don't believe the way those in class believe.* The room closed in on me with my mind attacking me and causing such negative feelings. I just wanted to run away. I couldn't wait for the class to finish, so I could leave. But God had something else in mind for me.

The teacher said, "I feel the anointing of healing. If anyone wants healing, come up and I'll lay hands on you." Everyone in the room ran to the front, while I stayed in my seat.

I have always struggled asking for help because it would make myself visible to others, and I wanted to stay invisible. Nevertheless, God showed He sees me, and there are times He will cause something to happen to make me even more visible.

I sat in my chair with my eyes closed but sensed someone come up behind me. I realized it was the teacher. He started praying for me. However, my mind only focused on someone praying for me; I didn't actually listen to his words. I know my spirit listened, not my physical ears. Fortunately, a friend heard every word and shared with me what the teacher said. He prayed for my entire nervous system, which seemed strange to me since my teacher only knew I had issues with my eyes. I drove home from class overwhelmed, but still wanting to drop this class and quit school completely. My thoughts continued to tell me: *Run away. You don't belong in this class nor the church.* It was the following day that my new health problem hit.

Saturday was an awful day, not only dreary with torrential rain and fog, but I felt like I was in a fight for my life. I couldn't function; my body and mind weren't working. I sat alone in my house, terrified. What could be happening? I'm not sure I can even articulate my symptoms. It felt like nothing in my body worked in a normal fashion. All I could handle was to sit in front of the TV hoping to be distracted and wishing my body and mind would return to normal.

During this strange new problem, noticing all my medical problems had worsened since I started attending Bible college and the church. I made a decision to quit both. If I hadn't known people at this church and been so visible, I would have easily not shown up. However, my friend Elisa attended, and several leaders in the church knew me personally, so it was hard to leave without saying goodbye and explaining my absence. God is so smart and knows me so well. He made sure in the short one year of attending this church that being known by the leaders and others would keep me from running. God perfectly placed me in this church with its church family so God would use them to help me become victorious in my journey. But this came only in hindsight.

The next day after my long and exhausting Saturday, I woke up determined to attend church for the last time and tell my friend I decided to quit everything as I couldn't take it anymore. What happened next was so interesting.

On this particular Sunday, Elisa didn't attend. This was extremely rare and had never happened for the year we'd been attending. So there I sat alone in the pew with my thoughts—just me and God. Minutes before the service began, Elisa's husband slipped quietly into the seat next to me. It was then our pastor did something different. Before the worship music, he came out to speak with us first. What he said startled me.

"I have a word for someone in the congregation. This person is about to give up and run, but the Lord is saying: 'Stand firm!'" Immediately Elisa's husband turned to me and said, "That is a word for *you*." How did he know? How did the pastor know? How did God know? I sat there in shock as well as moved by God's love.

I finally decided to share my emotional turmoil and new symptoms with Elisa and her husband. Prior to this Sunday, I could not have articulated these experiences because I thought I was losing my mind and others might think I was crazy. Both of them were great in helping me to understand I had an enemy who didn't want me to succeed in being healed and made whole. They helped me to strengthen my faith muscles and stand strong in the midst of my challenges, so I stayed in school and church. I recognized this experience as another major hurdle and milestone in my healing and faith journey with God. He wasn't finished yet. Another miracle happened.

Even though I didn't give up and ended up finishing my class, I now faced something more daunting. This was the first class since being healed of the brain injury where I had to tackle a final exam. I had taken many tests while living with the brain injury where I couldn't even understand the questions or answer questions correctly. My emotions were all over the place while taking the test, let alone completing it. This was a miracle. I couldn't believe what I had accomplished with God's help. Only a few short months before I couldn't even pay attention in class and now studying, retaining information, and recalling it at the time of the test was unbelievable. What was even more incredible, I received a test score of 99—only two incorrect answers. Not only did God bless me with the ability to study and take the test but enabled me to get an "A" on the exam. So what's next? I'm shooting for a 100!!!

A Giant Rainbow

A few months later as I drove to a midweek church service in recognition of college students, the pain in my eyes became worse triggering an intense migraine. The last thing I wanted to do was drive a car with my vision impaired. But I had a strong desire to be in God's house and didn't want to miss this particular church service as I was one of the college students being recognized.

As I drove I prayed to God saying, "You promised it was done and over, and I am standing on that promise!" It was more of a reminder to God what He had promised me at the beginning of the year when He said, "It is done and over." Within minutes of reminding God of His promise, an amazing thing happened.

A giant rainbow appeared right in front of my eyes. It was the largest one I had ever seen in my life and took up the entire sky on the highway I was driving on. While gasping at the magnitude and beauty of the rainbow, at that exact moment I heard God say in my spirit, "Here is my promise." Continuing to drive toward church, the rainbow grew bigger and bigger, and I knew it was given to me directly from God. It was His way of showing me during my pain He was still with me, would *never* leave me, and reassured me of my healing. Hebrews 13:5 tells us *For God has said,* "I will never fail you. I will never abandon you" (NLT).

Even more incredible, the rainbow didn't appear as a little arc, which you typically see off to the side of a road. Instead, taking over the entire sky, it appeared in my direct line of vision preventing me from having to turn to the left or right but keeping my eyes straight ahead. If I had moved my eyes even a little bit, the flashes in my eyes would have gone off, making the pain in my eyes even worse. The largeness of the rainbow made the event even more memorable by showing me how incredibly large God's heart is, how great and awesome His love is for each of us, and how He can express it through a rainbow.

Rainbows have always held a special place in my heart, and seeing one at this moment provided me with the strength to continue standing firm in God's promises and know all my symptoms would disappear.

The next three nights while out driving, God continued to strengthen me with rainbows. They weren't the same size as the first night and appeared almost like mini rainbows. I felt His presence so strongly and knew He had never left my side, especially during the challenging times dealing with all medical symptoms and other issues in my life.

One rainbow appeared while on my ride home from work. I saw three different colors peeking through the clouds. As soon as I saw it, it quickly vanished. Although just a quick glimpse, it enabled me to once again feel God's presence, despite having struggled for a couple of weeks, and know He still surrounded me. It kind of felt like He had given me a simple wink, that everything was okay. Having this same scene play out three nights in a row was God's way of strengthening me.

He also knew I have loved the story of Noah and the ark since childhood, especially where God told Noah He would never again flood the earth and wipe out mankind and provided the rainbow as His promise. While growing up, the rainbow always meant God's promise. So, seeing it that first day and thereafter, it turned out to be a perfect sign of His promise to me. In Genesis 9:13 and 17, God tells Noah and us, *I have placed my rainbow in the clouds. It is the sign of my covenant* (promise) (emphasis added) *with you and with all the earth. Yes, this rainbow is the sign of the covenant I am confirming with all the creatures on earth"* (NLT).

Locked Door

October 1, 2009, ushered in an interesting day. I had been struggling with pain in my chest, dizziness, and headaches, but continued to press on and walk by faith. I happened to be at my desk when a coworker friend walked into my office. I asked the familiar question, "How are you?" Instantly she said she wasn't feeling well and had a headache and felt dizzy. I listened to her tell me about her symptoms, and my spirit leaped inside of me. I knew I had to pray for her.

I shared God's Word about healing and asked her if I could pray for her. I prayed for her body and head, and immediately she said the pain in her head and numbness in her legs she had for almost a week were gone. We thanked God for her healing. I soon realized my own symptoms vanished at the same time.

I drove home from work that day, anxious to get there as my eyes had grown tired and I wanted to take out my contacts and put on my glasses. As I put the key into the lock to open my front door, the key didn't turn, and the door wouldn't open. My first thought? *You've got to be kidding.*

Immediately my mind raced. "This is the only way into my house. I need to take out my contacts. I'm going to be late for my night class." I quickly stopped this thinking and said, "No, Jesus can open this door." I began praying and asking Jesus to turn the key and open the door. Nothing happened. I thought, *Hmmm, strange, because I know He can open this door.* I tried again—nothing. I did not get anxious and thought, *I will call my friend and we'll pray together and it will open.* I called Elisa and there was no answer. I called another Christian friend and again I received no answer. I now turned to ask God for wisdom. "Why can't I get into my house?" I live in a condo, and there is only one way into the house; in addition, I knew it wasn't the key, so I couldn't call a locksmith. I put the key into the lock again, and it was then God revealed the reason to me.

I typically hung my book bag on the inside of the door on school nights as a reminder. This time was different as I had put my Bible in the book bag and it must have weighed down the door handle, preventing me from opening the door. I felt God say, "The enemy is using your Bible to lock you out of your house." That's when I really became annoyed. I said, "No way, this door is opening now!!!" The key moved, and the door opened.

What an amazing experience and another lesson in my life to show God is always with me and wants to help in all situations—even helping to release the pressure on a door handle.

Coworker's Little Girl

My job in the organization changed four times in 2009. Each time, it removed me from the people I worked with to a new environment and new team members. This latest reorganization in October brought me back to someone I had worked with before. Within a couple of weeks of working together, I found out her four-year-old daughter had come down with swine flu (H1N1), a very serious illness for a young child.

I sent her a note saying I would pray for her daughter and shared the healing scriptures I had come to embrace as a part of my life. I also told her I had sent a note to my Christian friends and there were many praying for her little girl.

The moment I sent an e-mail to my friends, we all began praying together and believing for total healing. Immediately the fever and symptoms her daughter had been experiencing disappeared, and she was on the road to total recovery. The timing of her daughter's healing was the moment we lifted her daughter up in our prayers. When speaking with my coworker, after she knew we prayed for her daughter, I shared with her about God's grace and how we all knew God wanted her daughter healed and whole. At that moment, it became apparent why I had been moved into this organization. When I originally moved to this team, I was not happy; however, I quickly realized God moved me and my friends there to intercede for this little girl and share with her Mom about God and His healing touch.

I now try to embrace organizational changes in a positive manner, recognizing they might be opening up opportunities where God can use me.

Needing a Breakthrough

While driving to a Wednesday night church service, I began experiencing tightness in my chest and labored breathing. I didn't want to give in to these feelings, so as I set out to drive to church,

I began singing. With tears streaming down my face, I sang my made-up song for the entire twenty-minute drive to church:

> My breakthrough is coming, my breakthrough is here, my breakthrough is coming because of my Lord.

During the worship service, my breathing became shallow, feeling like something was blocking me from being able to take a breath. I also had trouble standing. So, for the first time, I sat down to worship. All I could say was "Jesus." I kept saying His name over and over. By this time, my hands were sweating, and I knew I needed help or I wouldn't get through the service or the rest of the night.

Before worship ended, one of the elders said, "I believe someone needs a breakthrough." I cried, knowing it was me who needed the breakthrough. I am continually blown away how God speaks to me at exact times, especially when I'm in a desperate situation.

After service, I ran into my friend Cathy who had been sharing with me about healing and mentioned to her about these latest symptoms. Her counsel to me? "Walk by faith." When I mentioned how dizzy I felt and I wasn't sure how I could drive home, her response again was "Drive by faith."

Those words echoed in my head in the weeks and months to come, as many times I had to drive my car by faith. I don't know what caused these symptoms that night, but I knew and felt God's presence so strong. He carried me through the night and gave me the ability to drive my car home.

The above are all examples of God's grace and mercy, showing how much He wants to take care of us and help us through all aspects of our lives. These moments are what strengthened my faith muscles and enabled me to continue, although my incredible journey with God wasn't over yet.

CHAPTER 5

An Incredible Year!

A new year meant another incredible journey was about to begin. By the end of the year, I hoped to look back to see how much my faith muscles were exercised and strengthened—but what would it take?

Fasting for a Breakthrough

January began with our pastor teaching about "Fasting for Breakthroughs" as a congregation. While we learned about different ways to fast, for me it would not be a total fast from food, but eating fruits and vegetables similar to what is called the Daniel Fast. I thought this could be a challenge for someone like me who really didn't like to eat many foods, except for junk food and sweets. Intrigued during each week's sermon about fasting, I felt the Holy Spirit was preparing me to participate in this experience. My biggest concern was what to eat. Further, I also wanted to increase my faith for the healing manifestation of the medical symptoms concerning my eyes and the other crazy symptoms I had been living with for more than two years.

As I learned more and more about the fast, I couldn't wait to get started. I wanted and needed breakthroughs in my life—not only with God but also with my eyes. We learned some leadership individuals were participating in a 40-day fast and others thirty-one days. The entire congregation was asked to join in only a 21-day fast. I thought I should be able to do it for that long, so I began to prepare.

I searched the internet on the types of food I could eat during this time of fasting. But as I prepared my heart for this new journey, I realized that limiting my food wouldn't be my biggest sacrifice. God placed in my heart that I should also "fast" TV. Now, that would be a sacrifice. Yet, I reasoned it would give me more time to spend with God and draw closer to him—which I learned was the whole idea behind the fast. I know many don't believe giving up something like TV is considered "fasting" and believe you need to deny your body of "rich" food and sweets, but for me denying this type of food would have been easy and not considered a sacrifice.

I looked at the calendar to see when the twenty-one days began when I realized the Winter Olympics would occur smack in the middle of the fast. Being a *huge* sports fan and loving the Winter Olympics, I thought: *Wow! This is really a sacrifice!* I knew my normal routine of being glued to the TV was about to change and a new opportunity of spending time with God about to surface. As the weeks approached for us to begin our corporate fast, I suddenly felt the urge to begin fasting earlier than scheduled after attending a Sunday church. I already had the right food in the house, and when I came home from church that Sunday, I never turned on the TV. When I realized Super Bowl Sunday was the following Sunday, I thought, *Oh boy, my first challenge. Will I be able to* not *watch it? Will I cave in and turn it on?*

However, my first challenge came only three days into the fast, before Super Bowl Sunday. In the middle of the night, I awoke to severe pains in my stomach. I broke out in a sweat and was dizzy as I walked to the bathroom. I was sick for a couple of hours, and I could hear the thoughts swirling in my head, *You really can't do this fast. Look. It's making you sick. You aren't going to be able to do this!*

I panicked, wondering what I did to my body. Obviously, it was rejecting the food I was fasting on, and I didn't have the TV to help distract me through the night. I felt totally alone in my room and then thought, *Wait a minute—Daniel in the Bible got stronger and was healthy while he ate the same food I'm eating.* I immediately fought back my negative thoughts and instead started speaking out loud: "I am getting stronger and healthier just like Daniel. I am putting good and healthy food into my body."

The next day, weak and feeling dizzy, I spoke to a friend who also attended our church. She reassured me my body could be detoxing and I should be okay soon. I continued with the Daniel Fast (eating fruits and vegetables) and no TV. By the end of the first week, my previous brain injury symptoms tried to reappear—dizziness, confusion, trouble concentrating, and pain and pressure inside my head. I was so glad our pastor prepared us to anticipate physical problems and said we must "stand firm" against them. I immediately recognized this to be a test—a test to continue and see if I really believed I had been healed of the brain injury and could be healed of the remaining medical issues. I passed the test, knowing these symptoms that reappeared were not going to be a part of my life anymore, and they left within a couple of days. I "stood firm" in my faith!

After the first week, something interesting and awesome happened. A family member reached out to me for help and over the next couple of days continued to share with me little things like a video clip or an event on TV. I shared this with Elisa who was also participating in the fast, and she pointed out to me there was a connection. All this time, I was believing for the manifestation of the healing of my body, and God had other plans—for healing a personal relationship. What an incredible experience! Since the fast, this relationship had been restored, and I was able to provide the help this person needed. We didn't speak about the past. It wasn't necessary. I can only attribute this reconciliation to God.

A New England Cruise in September

A new opportunity surfaced in the coming months when I heard about a ten-day cruise to New England. The cruise, sponsored by a local Christian radio station, included a senior pastor and several local pastors.

It sounded perfect, and I was always ready to go on a cruise. I was now two years into living as a healed brain injury survivor, yet with new physical symptoms and my eyes not yet healed but anticipating the day of the manifestation. With this cruise, I jumped at any opportunity to go out into the world and live life to the fullest. I had already managed one cruise to Alaska and was about to now venture on my second, only to a different destination. Traveling alone in a safe group is a great experience. It gives you the freedom to be yourself and meet new people while trying experiences you might not do if traveling with friends and family. But something else happened I didn't expect, and neither did any of the other passengers.

The first two days, the sea became extremely rough due to a tornado hitting the port the day we departed. Our cruise ship left about an hour earlier than expected because of pending weather. We later learned a fierce storm had been forecasted which caused us to leave earlier than planned and at a faster speed. As everyone stood at the helm of the ship at the beginning of our new adventure, we could see the tremendous storm clouds approaching. The ship moved at a rapid pace through the channel and under the Verrazano Bridge (in New York City). I had sailed under this bridge many times before, however not at this speed. Shortly after departing came the standard boat drill. It was moved inside for safety—another sign something was happening outside normal routine.

Next on the agenda was dinner and we noticed the window shades had been pulled completely down. Several of us were curious and peeked under the shades near our table only to see waves covering the windows, definitely not typical. The seas were experiencing a severe and unusual storm. Within a few short minutes, the captain spoke over the loud speaker.

"Ladies and gentlemen, a tornado just hit and damaged the port where we left. Let me reassure you the carport where most of you parked your vehicles remains untouched. Everyone's cars are safe."

The majority of people in this Christian group were from the same church, and they had already paired up and were traveling together. It is challenging for me to introduce myself and jump into already existing groups, so I figured I'd ask God for help since I didn't know anyone. I prayed for open opportunities to meet someone who would befriend me.

The opportunity came the very next day while playing miniature golf. I met a lady who introduced me to the rest of the individuals traveling. It only takes one person to make a difference. We swapped stories from our lives and what God had been doing and, of course, my story, being healed of a traumatic brain injury. I shared how the sky is the limit for me and I wanted to do and try new experiences now. My new group of friends encouraged me to climb the rock wall on the top of the cruise ship. Since I had expressed a desire and a couple of them were planning to try, I decided to join in. Before my brain injury, there wasn't anything I couldn't do physically. Now healed, I believed I had that same ability again!

The night before the rock climbing event, we were sharing stories at the dinner table; and my healing story, of course, came up. There were a couple of pastors present while I shared my testimony. You could have heard a pin drop. The pastors were amazed and thrilled at my story, and then the ladies told about my plan to climb the rock wall the next day. Everyone was now in my corner thrilled to see me ready to do this.

Oh boy, I started to feel the pressure of doing the actual climb. In the past I had no fear, but since the brain injury, fear had crept into my daily life. *Can I really do this? Do I have the physical strength as well as the nerve it takes to climb?* Not only did I need to prove this to myself, but now the pastors and their church members were coming to see me climb.

With a gorgeous blue sky overhead, we signed the paperwork and put on our climbing shoes. Excited about getting started, the pastors and my new friends took their place to watch, and one person came with a camera ready to capture this historic moment.

Awaiting my turn in line, I processed how far I had come over the past couple of years, from sitting on the sofa with pain in my head looking out at the world to standing on the twelfth floor of a cruise ship looking up at a wall I was about to climb. In my first book, *From Night to Light*, I explained how, after suffering the traumatic brain injury, I believed one day I would climb a mountain. Now, I was only moments away from doing that—not really an actual mountain, but to me I was about to make a physical climb that would truly test me.

The instructor called me over to the ropes. I stressed my concerns to him. "Please don't let me fall. I was just healed of a brain injury, and any help you can give me to reach the top will be greatly appreciated." He answered, "Don't worry. I'm here for you."

Emotions flooded me as I took my first step on the wall, not only realizing how far I've come but also aware of the huge group cheering me on to victory. With each step, I heard their excited cheers below me.

Climbing the wall was much harder than I expected. Your face is pressed against the wall, and you can't see where to put your hands or feet. I had to rely on the instructor below telling me which hand and foot to move. Okay, so now I needed to know my right from my left. Years ago this had been a challenge.

Making my way slowly up the rock wall, I noticed a halfway spot where you could ring a bell before proceeding to the upper level of the rock wall. As I reached the halfway bell, I rang it loud and proudly, deciding not to go any further. By reaching this first bell, I felt I had already hit a huge accomplishment and didn't want to overexert myself as it could impact the rest of my trip. In my heart, of course, I wanted to go all the way to the top, but the overachiever in me needed to learn about this new brain and body, any possible limitations, and know when to quit. Instead of looking at it as a failure by not going to the top, I appreciated my achievement of making it to the halfway point. I saw it as a major accomplishment.

When I climbed down, I overheard one of the pastors telling the watching crowd I had been healed of a brain injury. People were amazed at this considerable achievement. Isn't it wonderful the unique places where we can witness and show others God's miracles and love? Can you believe just years ago I not only had trouble walking but even making it up slight inclines? Now, I had just climbed a rock wall on top of a cruise ship! Absolutely amazing.

One of my new friends had planned a whale-watching excursion and had been praying to see at least one whale. I agreed with her in prayer that she would see many whales and told her we could ask

God to speak to the whales since God spoke to the whale, or big fish, in the Bible story about Jonah. I couldn't wait to hear about her trip when she returned. When she did, she reported how overwhelmed she was at the many whales they saw and showed me pictures and a video. It was absolutely amazing. God had delivered.

Sitting on my balcony before getting ready for dinner, I wished I had gone on the whale excursion with her and then suddenly thought, *Well, if God can speak to the whales out in the ocean, He could surely bring a dolphin right outside my ocean-view balcony.* I began praying. Within an instant, three dolphins jumped out of the water and swam alongside the ship. How amazing is our God. We just need to speak to Him and ask, and as a precious Father He delivers. I sat for a while watching these dolphins swim alongside just for me and thanked God for all the blessings and the incredible life journey He has given me.

The next morning I felt lazy and wanted to stay in bed. I lay there recalling one of my goals was to get up early to see the sunrise. Immediately, I heard God speaking to me, "Get out of bed. I've given you this great ocean view!" I quickly jumped out of bed, opened my sliding glass door, and stepped out onto my balcony. I looked out to an incredible sunrise and unbelievable view. I grabbed my camera and snapped beautiful photos. In the far-off distance, I saw a sailboat and the sun peeking over the horizon. My thoughts turned to how massive the sun looked compared to the small sailboat. At that moment, I felt God showed me just how big His *Son* (Jesus) really is. What a remarkable experience as I stood on my balcony and took in God's power and glory, feeling overwhelmingly blessed. If I had been lazy and slept in, I would have missed this beautiful moment.

God had blessed me so many times with opportunities and special experiences. I needed to continue to keep my eyes focused on Him so none of these precious moments would ever slip by.

Cookies and Soda

God can even use cookies and soda to enable us to overcome challenges in our lives. I had been invited to my first Impact Group (small Bible study group in church members' homes) on a Wednesday evening sponsored by our church. While still not comfortable committing to anything because of all my weird symptoms with my eyes, I knew I needed to commit myself to go. I'd like to say I knew it was by the Holy Spirit's prompting—and it was—but I don't think I knew it at the time.

My hostess for the Impact Group was Cathy, the teacher from the women's conference and someone special God had placed in my life; therefore when she invited me, I knew I needed to attend and do whatever I was asked. I offered to bake chocolate chip cookies, and Cathy asked if I could also bring soda. Three days prior to this first get-together, I developed a migraine in both eyes. The pain grew worse, making it a struggle to keep my eyes open and work on my computer. I kept wondering how I could drive an hour to the Impact Group. In the last fifteen years, I had never really driven this kind of distance, especially with the flashes now occurring in my eyes. What is so incredible about God is He knows each of us so well. He knew the commitment I had made to bake cookies and bring soda would keep me from canceling.

The big day arrived, and I had my GPS system programmed and the route mapped out for a distance of about fifty minutes without traffic. As I set out for my drive, it started to rain; and I thought, *You've got to be kidding. I'm already nervous about driving, and I still have a migraine in both eyes.* Sitting in bumper-to-bumper traffic I hadn't planned on, the words coming out of my mouth were, "I can't do this. This is too hard. I'm never doing this again. Cathy is just going to have to understand this is too far for me to travel." On and on went my negative thoughts.

Halfway on my drive, I had a light bulb moment as I listened to the negative words coming out of my mouth. Typically, I try hard to only speak and think positive and encouraging thoughts, so I fought against these negatives and began speaking God's Words: "I have been healed. There is nothing wrong with my eyes. My eyes are strong and healthy. They were healed when Jesus went to the cross for me. God restored my brain. He gave me the ability to drive this car."

I thanked and praised God for all the healing He had done in my life and claimed victory over my eyes, my body, and even the ability to drive. While the migraine and rain didn't go away, I felt stronger internally and knew I had achieved victory.

At Cathy's house, we opened with a worship song. Cathy's daughter played the guitar and led us in worship. My initial thought, *Oh no, my head is vibrating! That guitar is so loud! Do we have to sing?* Of course, God is so good and used Sarah to lead us in a song about healing, one of my favorites. As we sang, the migraine I had experienced for three days completely vanished, and the pain just melted away. *Amen!!!*

We had a great time of worship and teaching. I met new people and was asked to share my testimony of being healed of the brain injury. God continues to open up opportunities for me to share my testimony and His story. I also explained the challenge I experienced while driving to the Impact Group. Amazing how the story of my challenge with the migraines and driving problems affected and helped those who attended the group.

Feeling blessed and honored because God used me to help others, I began my drive home. There were no flashes in my eyes. This was the *very* first time in more than three years I didn't experience lightning bolt flashes while in a car at night. The entire hour drive home, flash free, proved to be another incredible experience. God used cookies and sodas to get me back into my car that night and overcome my anxiety about driving especially at night.

Since that experience, I felt more confident about driving at night and have even driven to several locations more than an hour in distance. God enabled me to have a victory that night, and I know my faith in God's Word equipped me with what I needed. If I hadn't stepped out in faith, I might never have gotten back in the car to drive at night.

What an incredible year this has been! What might the coming years entail, since the two years after being healed from the brain injury have already been an incredible experience?

What was next for me?

CHAPTER 6

Victory while in School

What came next was learning to trust in God and being victorious while returning back to school.

It sounded like a daunting experience because my doctors told me I would never be able to go back to school as I didn't have the ability to learn anything new because of the brain injury.

Then, in April of 2008, my friend Elisa invited me to a Bible class (this was one month prior to hearing the healing teaching.) Her church had opened a Bible college, and she was anxious to attend the first semester. When she asked, I thought, *How could I attend a three-hour class while struggling with a brain injury?* Of course, she had all the answers—it would be a Saturday class, so I didn't have to worry about driving after work or in the evening. The session started in the morning, so I had the afternoon to rest. I could audit the class which meant I only had to show up and didn't have to do the homework, participate, or take any tests.

On the surface, her input sounded good; however, doing anything new always had its challenges. I agreed to attend but then went into my typical *what ifs*:

What if I look dumb in class?

What if the teacher calls on me for an answer and I don't understand the question?

What if I get overly tired in the classroom and find myself struggling?

Lucky for me, Elisa sat right beside me and agreed to handle anything thrown in my direction. Isn't it great how God provides us with the exact people in our lives as we are besieged in our journey?

This was our first Bible class, and we were excited to be together and learn more about God. The class syllabus indicated homework; and, of course, my initial reaction was panic! Elisa had to remind me again. Auditing the class would not require me to actually do anything.

The first homework assignment consisted of writing a page or two about a specific disciple and answering a few questions. I decided to give it a try.

It was difficult for me to comprehend the material and the questions, let alone write in my own words a summary of each question and answer. I also had to provide an overview of the disciple assigned for that week. I ran my ideas by Elisa, and she helped me organize my thoughts so I could write them clearly. I handed in my paper. God is so faithful. He guided and helped me complete the weekly assignments. After getting my first paper back with an "A," I thought, *Wow, maybe I can do this!*

I feared another dilemma. The teacher's style in class was interactive. He called on people on the spur of the moment. I was in deep water with this one. I knew if he called on me in class to answer a question, I might not be able to think clearly or quickly enough. Therefore, I felt I needed to open up to the teacher about my brain injury. I wrote him a note to help him understand my challenges, so he wouldn't be too surprised if I appeared to be struggling and would be aware that my brain might, at times, zone out. Also, if he called my name, I might give the impression of not paying attention or might not even respond. Letting him know of my limitations instead of trying to hide my disability took the pressure off.

He was more than accommodating and I think took a special interest to encourage me to succeed. With each of my homework papers receiving an "A," I gained confidence in delivering a good paper each time, even though it did take me the entire weekend to produce only a one-page document. The pain in my head and the physical exhaustion were worth getting an "A" each week.

Halfway through the course, the dean and my teacher approached me about taking this class for credit so I could start working toward a "Certificate in Biblical Studies." I went into shock. *No way*, I thought. How could I take tests and hand in papers like everyone else? For some reason I agreed, probably because the first class had gone so well and partly because I didn't fully understand what I was agreeing to. Many times I just said yes to people's questions or comments. Then, I realized a final exam would have to be taken at the end of the course, and my mind quickly filled with doubt. How could I study and retain information for a test? The answer came, based on having so many previous experiences with God. He would be there with me. And so would Elisa.

A week or two before the end of the semester, I sat in class pondering whether to take the final exam. When I looked at my notes, there were words, but they made no sense and looked like stuff scribbled all over the pages. When living with a brain injury, one's thoughts get jumbled. Between the time I heard and tried to process what the teacher had said and the time I wrote it on my paper, there were gaps, and the content was lost in translation. It seemed as if words were just haphazardly plopped onto a piece of paper.

I said to myself maybe if the teacher made it an open book test, I would consider taking the exam. Within seconds of my thoughts, the teacher said to the class, "I've never done this before, but I feel I should make this test open book." As the class cheered, I sat in amazement thinking the teacher had read my thoughts. How could that be? I learned later it was all God. In addition, I also had a secret weapon, my friend Elisa who is the best notetaker I have ever met. Each week she provided me with copies of her notes. I could use them when taking the test.

Test day arrived, and my nerves were in high gear. Would I be able to read the test questions and understand them enough to be able to find the answer either in my notes, in Elisa's notes, or from the open book? We had the entire three-hour class period to take the exam. Elisa was finished in less than thirty minutes. I think I might have completed an answer or two in that same timeframe. As the clock ticked, my anxiety increased, feeling like I couldn't really do this. However, even though Elisa was finished, she sat next to me the entire time encouraging me and believing I could finish this test.

I took forever. I needed the entire three hours to complete the exam. By the end, there were only the three of us left in the classroom—the teacher, Elisa, and me. While totally exhausted, I did feel a level of accomplishment, and I know Elisa and my teacher were proud of my being able to finish the test. I didn't know it at the time, but I do now. God was there with me encouraging and helping me take the exam.

God always wants to bless His children. I ended up with a 96 on my final exam. How great is that for a straight A high school and college student to get a 96 in her first Bible college course while dealing with a brain injury? This would be the first A in a long line of As that would come as I continued taking Bible classes. I proved the doctors wrong when they said I couldn't go back to school and learn anything new.

During the next school semester, the fall of 2008, I had to take the class alone. Elisa couldn't attend. I guess God felt I could handle this alone after being helped during the first class. I believe God sometimes nudges His children out of their comfort zone to grow and stretch their faith muscles and leave their "spiritual mothers and fathers," which is how I viewed Elisa. Over the years, I had felt these nudges many times before, and each time I saw growth at the end of the nudge. I learned I am never really alone; God is always there. In addition to God's help, during this upcoming class, Elisa's husband happened to be in the building at the same time, so he routinely checked in on me. The teacher for this class was our church's worship leader who was already familiar with my situation and was extremely helpful and attentive.

Toward the end of the course and right before the final exam, I experienced my healing miracle of the brain injury! This miracle is discussed in the early chapters of this book as well as in my first book, *From Night to Light.*

When it came time to take the final exam, my emotions were all over the place because of my healing. I took the day off to study and go over my notes. How exciting! I had the ability to study and actually recall what I read as well!

I drove to school, excited to take the exam, but also a little nervous. The test started, and when I turned over the paper and saw the first question, it was an awesome feeling because I immediately knew the answer. I quickly moved to question 2, and again the answer came. I wrote it down hoping it wouldn't disappear from my thoughts like it had done for so many years before. With each turn of the page, my excitement increased as I read the question and wrote down the answer. Tears fell from my eyes and dropped on the paper as God showed me with each answer my brain had been fully restored. God gave me an incredible miracle. When I handed in the paper, I think my smile must have been from ear to ear.

Before starting my car to drive home, I called Elisa to share with her how I had answered all the questions and completed the test knowing I did well. Not only could I answer the questions but knew I gave the correct answers. There might have been one or two questions I wasn't completely sure of, but I knew I didn't fail this test like I had failed all the neurological tests a few years earlier. Elisa was just as excited as I was, and we were even more thrilled when I opened the results a week later showing a score of 99. How amazing is that—a girl who struggled to remember her address now received almost a perfect score on her first test paper. God is so great!

In three short years, I earned enough credits to receive my "Certificate in Biblical Studies" and, even more amazing, graduated with a 4.0 average. I received an "A" in each class, and in eight out of thirteen classes, I scored a perfect 100 on the tests and final grade. God not only enabled me to achieve. He equipped me to excel. In one of the classes, I even created two electronic Jeopardy games, and the teacher had me facilitate the game during two of our classes since I knew the material so well. Most of the students had no idea I had recently been healed of a brain injury. The teacher indicated he believed he would one day see me teach the entire class.

The Bible tells us God will restore what the enemy stole from us. In Joel 2:25, the Lord says, *So, I will restore to you the years that the swarming locust has eaten…* (NKJV). While I thought I had lost my ability to think and learn, both had been completely restored, and my ability to process, think, and learn has exceeded my expectations.

While I had always dreamed of getting my master's degree in business, God had other plans for me, even more than I could have hoped to achieve. He changed my heart and passion from continuing education in the business world to now focusing on how God could use me to help others, by sharing my many healing testimonies and teaching what God has taught me.

Learning to trust in Him was the best decision of my life. What could be next?

CHAPTER 7

I AM Covering and Protecting Your Head

O God the Lord, the strength of my salvation. You covered my head in the day of battle. (Psalm 140:7)

Sunday, January 9, 2011, started out as every other Sunday, or so I thought when I sat quietly talking with God before the beginning of the church service.

Normally, I always ask Him to protect and guide me as my journey continues with its challenges and struggles and to give me patience while waiting for the symptoms to completely leave my body. I had no doubt God had always been at my side during each challenging journey; however, many times these experiences were tiring and exhausting, and I now felt I was reaching the end of my rope. I was weary of the pain and wanted my body to work correctly.

Yes, I had been completely healed of the brain injury, but I still had lightning bolt flashes and large spots in my eyes with lingering pain in both eyes and body; and now, a strange burning smell was causing me to have trouble breathing. These experiences were discouraging. So, as I sat quietly with God, this particular Sunday I did something different.

I asked God for a "fresh encounter" with Him, not even knowing for sure what I was asking, for I don't ever recall hearing anyone use that phrase, or could it be something the Holy Spirit placed in my heart?

Just as service began, the lights in the church dimmed for a beautiful time of worship. I had my eyes closed to help me draw closer to God. We sang one song when I heard what sounded like my name being called. My eyes burst wide open. *Who could be calling me?* I quickly looked at Elisa, standing next to me. She stared back at me with the same surprised expression. What happened next felt like slow motion and a long duration, but I'm sure it lasted only a few minutes.

"Donna. Where is Donna?" When I opened my eyes, it was the pastor standing at the front of the altar. There were several hundred people in attendance and I'm sure more than one Donna, but somehow I knew immediately he meant me. Now this was unusual as our pastor typically delivered his sermon *after* our time of worship. He explained he didn't mean to disrupt worship, but what he had to say was a form of worshipping God.

He called me to the front, and in a panic I asked my friend, "Do I really have to go up there?"

Elisa answered me by moving into the aisle to make room for me to pass and make my way up to the front of the church. It felt like the Red Sea parting as I walked from my second row seat to the front with members who were worshipping there moving aside to clear a direct path for me. A light appeared to be drawing me toward my pastor who stood waiting for me to join him at the altar. The light was so real I believed the lighting crew had turned up the lights at the altar but purposely left the lights in the audience dim. All I know was I felt led to follow the light.

My insides were shaking. I don't like surprises and typically want to know what is happening in advance so I can be prepared. I was now out of my comfort zone but totally in the hands of my Lord.

Pastor began explaining to the congregation. God had provided him with a scripture to share with me, which he typically shared in private and at the end of a service. However, God encouraged him to do it during the service.

I stood in front of him, my head swirling. *What is happening*, I thought, *and what does this mean?* I tried to pay attention to every word he was saying so I could later ask my friend what just happened. The scripture God provided to the pastor was *Psalm 140:7—O GOD the Lord, the strength of my salvation, thou hast covered my head in the day of battle* (KJV). They posted the scripture on the screen. I had never read it or heard it before, so my brain tried to quickly read and process its meaning.

Pastor, with tears filling his eyes, put his arm on my shoulder, his full attention only on me. In that moment I lost all awareness we were standing in front of hundreds of people. It felt like the two of us were the only two people in a private world. His face was full of compassion.

"I don't know all what you are going through," he said, "but God does and He wanted you to have this scripture."

I know he said much more; however, I felt my brain was not processing or retaining everything he said. But one thing I am completely sure of, my spirit heard every word!

Pastor then placed his hands on my head and prayed for me. Unfortunately, I don't remember his prayer but, again, my spirit heard it. It seemed like my body went limp and I fell backward into the arms of an usher standing behind me. I understand this sometimes happens when God's presence is so strong it can be too much to handle and physically you are overwhelmed not only with emotions but also the power of God. I'm not sure I can explain all that happened, but I can tell you it was a powerful experience and one I will never forget.

After a few moments I got up. The service had continued, and people were worshipping and singing to God. I found my way back to my seat with tears streaming down my face and reached the open arms of my friend Elisa. She is the person God chose to guide me through this journey, from the point of my receiving the revelation of my brain injury healing to every miracle and special moment in my journey with God.

I cried through the entire church service, emotionally spent afterward. I immediately wanted to know more about this experience. I'm one of those people who needs to understand everything. Yet, strangely, God has put in my life lots of "feelers," people who are led by emotions rather than their thoughts. Elisa's words to me, as a "feeler," were "Just enjoy the gift." But I didn't understand the gift and kept pondering and asking questions. *What does this scripture mean? Why did pastor call me out in the middle of church? Why did this happen?*

I spent the rest of Sunday reading Psalm 140:7 in different Bible versions—the King James, New King James, New Living Translation, and the Amplified Bible. Each version was slightly different and providing me with details to help piece this message from God together. I asked God, "What are you trying to show me? What do I need to understand?"

I didn't get an answer that day, so I tried to do what Elisa said. Just enjoy the gift and experience.

The next day at work, I met up with my pastor's daughter who worked in the same organization. She smiled at me, and we both said, "Wow, that was an interesting service." She shared with me her dad had never done that before in all his thirty years of preaching. Now I was even more curious to find out. *Why me?* I couldn't wait to go home and spend time with God again so He could reveal to me what all of this meant.

At home, I quietly sat with God and spoke the words again, "God, I need a fresh encounter with you." Then, it hit me. Those were the words I spoke on Sunday morning before service began—look what happened! So do you think there is a connection? Of course there is!

God wanted to show me how big His love is for me. Until this time, I didn't really understand God as a Father and His love for me as a daughter. To me, the word "love" was just a four-letter word with no depth or meaning, so I never really felt it. Reflecting back on Sunday morning and recalling my pastor's eyes filled with compassion, love, and tears and his placing his hand on my shoulder and speaking softly to me, I saw how this exactly modeled a father's love for His daughter. Instantly God had used him to relay His love as my Father and how much He cared for me.

I believe God orchestrated this dramatic moment publicly to demonstrate to me how He indeed loves me. He called me out from my seat in the dark and brought me to the front of the room into the light not only to show me how special I am to Him but for everyone to see.

Psalm 140:7 now made sense. Not only had God protected my head during the brain injury but also protected my mind and thoughts. God knew the latter was very necessary, as I am the type who is always thinking, and during these years my mind continued to be attacked with negative thoughts, *You'll never get well. You don't really matter. You can't really work anymore.* These negative thoughts were endless since the injury, and I no longer had confidence personally or at work like I had prior to the accident. All my crazy medical symptoms kept me believing the lies that I would never fully recover, and some of these symptoms might even take my life.

My experience or "fresh encounter" with God brought me to an even deeper relationship with Him. Now I can come to Him as a daughter comes to her father. He is not only my Creator but also my Father who wants only the best for me. Understanding now, His love gives me the bravery to handle the challenges and struggles I still face and the courage to "stand by faith" in the battles lying ahead in the months and years to come.

CHAPTER 8

Stepping Out in Faith

My next battle occurred in 2012. I knew I had been healed four years earlier of the brain injury and nothing was wrong with my body or brain, but old ways of thinking die hard. This was especially so when it concerned long distance traveling on my own. My first panicky experience with this occurred back in 2006 when a French organization bought the company I worked for. What happened then had a great bearing on how I coped with what happened to me in 2012.

When the French company bought our company in 2006, it had been met with mixed emotions. Some employees saw a great opportunity for free trips to France, while others saw only the changes there would be. I too had mixed emotions. I didn't like change; nevertheless, I set out to embrace these new challenges.

Throughout the several years working for this French-owned company, opportunities surfaced for me to travel to Paris. While this might sound exciting and you might say, "Lucky you," I panicked each time my boss wanted me in Paris. The conversation went something like this: "Donna, I need you at a meeting in Paris" My response? "Okay." Then the internal dialogue in my head began.

"Oh my gosh, I can't travel to Paris. The flight is too long. What if my body and brain don't work while in flight or while in Paris? I can't work all day, go out to dinner in the evening with coworkers, and then get up or work in the morning."

These negative thoughts increased until I reached a state of panic. You see, I wanted people to believe there was nothing wrong with me and my brain and body functioned normally like everyone else. As a reminder, in 2006, my brain had not been completely healed, and I still had to deal with crazy symptoms and a physical body not strong enough to travel.

With every request for me to travel to Paris, I immediately prayed and sought God. I knew He was the source of my strength and the best judge of whether my physical body could handle this type of trip. Miraculously, each time before we had to book the trip, it was canceled for one reason or another; and I felt a great sense of relief. I also chuckled, knowing God had played a role in the cancelation, aware I wasn't physically or mentally ready to travel. While part of me loved the idea of traveling to Paris and seeing the sights and new experiences, the other part of me was in total trepidation realizing it might become evident to my coworkers I wasn't the perfect healthy person I pretended to be each day. Many of my coworkers knew about my brain injury; however, the majority didn't know of my daily challenges and struggles.

The years passed; my job and organizations changed, and there were no more requests to travel to Paris.

Then 2012 happened.

I had been asked to support a new project where employees based in Vimercate, Italy, needed to change the way they currently worked. Since our company struggled financially, travel had always been discouraged, and I had felt safe. I wouldn't be required to travel and could remain in New Jersey. My role in this new project, however, required my supporting these employees, by communicating through letters, e-mails, or newsletters and ensuring they were trained efficiently. I could still handle this type of support from my base location.

Nearing the "go live" of this new system and process, we were experiencing issues at our Vimercate location as well as our Plano, Texas, location. My boss approached me.

"Donna, I need you in Italy." My heart sunk, but I quietly said, "Okay."

I believe he knew about my brain injury and seemed to know intuitively I didn't like to travel, so he followed up with the question, "Are you okay to travel?" I told him "Yes."

While others in our organization leaped at the opportunity to travel, I never raised my hand or took advantage of these opportunities. You see, I knew God was aware I couldn't travel, and He would find a way to cancel any trip I was scheduled for like He had done so many times before. I said "Yes" to my boss because I didn't want to come across as "cowardly" by saying I couldn't go. Therefore, I confidently said yes, knowing I could leave it in God's Hands.

The days approached for my final travel plans to be made, but nothing appeared to be stopping the trip or canceling it like all the other times. I started having conversations with God to make Him aware He needed to cancel this trip quickly as the time was approaching fast. My quiet time with God, however, left me with the feeling He wasn't about to do so, leaving me to think maybe there was some reason I needed to make this trip. God knew at this time I had already been healed of the brain injury and was healthy and strong and had the physical ability to make the excursion. Nevertheless, I struggled to believe I could do it. Worse yet, all indications pointed to my having to travel to Italy *alone.*

At first, I thought this had to be a mistake, as I had never traveled to another country alone or even to another state by myself since the accident. My initial emotion was of apprehension; but I quickly realized God wanted me to take this journey, and if God had confidence I could make this trip, then I needed to align my thinking with His and believe I was completely capable.

I decided to go to the Plano, Texas, location first as a way to get my *travel feet* and get a sense of what to expect workwise when I went to Italy. The job required at both of these locations is called "user acceptance testing," where the employees do a test run of the new system we were installing, using trial and error methodology. I had never experienced this type of assignment and believed seeing it through with American users might be a good test run for me before traveling to meet my Italian colleagues.

Overall, the trip proved to be a great experience. I flew alone, rented a car, and drove myself to the hotel. While this sounds easy for most people, you need to remember this was the first time since being healed of the brain injury. Previously, I needed someone to do everything for me. Many times after being healed, doing little things on my own for the first time was a huge challenge. Think back to the first time you traveled alone or did something for the very first time. It's kind of scary. Yet, after completing it, you gain so much confidence and feel great. It initially felt scary, traveling to Plano. I felt like a teenager driving a car for the first time on a road trip. I made it safely to the hotel, checked in, found my room, and knew I had conquered a huge milestone, but there was another one to tackle.

My next milestone was sitting in an all-day meeting for the entire week in the presence of new faces and being able to process something new that I was learning. This was tough because it was my job to understand new information. So, if I didn't fully understand something, I had to find creative ways to hide that lack of unknowingness so my bosses wouldn't assume I had any deficiency with my brain. Since the injury, even though now healed, I still didn't have the confidence in my job abilities. I lived each day, fearful someone would think I wasn't performing to full capacity as I did before the injury. In essence, I wasn't perfect. A lot of this was, of course, in my head, as made evident by my bosses continually reassuring me my job performance excelled and they considered me an expert in my area. However, I believed I didn't work to the degree I did before the accident.

Each day in Plano I gained more and more confidence. My ability to pay attention in meetings, connect the dots to what the employees needed to understand, and even answer questions that were out of my scope all began to feel natural. I was performing at the level I used to before the accident!

The entire week proved to be a success, not only for me personally but also for the company's working environment. At the beginning of the week, the employees had resisted the change we were recommending; however, by the end of the week, the Plano team was now in full support, and their leader even agreed to travel with us to

Italy to share how much he felt the new system and process would benefit the Italian team. My boss was thrilled with the outcome and glad I had suggested going to Plano first.

I felt great having taken this trip for me personally, as well as professionally, as it gave me confidence in my working ability and equipped me to take on the next challenge of traveling to Italy. But first I struggled with the thoughts of having to get on a plane and travel six hours in the air. Was I even going to be able to get on that plane?

My answer came when I reached out to a particular elder at my church. He had prayed for me before when I had to fly while living with my crazy medical symptoms. I remember his words asking God to release His angels to encamp around me, and I kept those words close in my heart. He told me he and the other elders would be in prayer for me throughout the trip, and I knew I was in great hands.

The flight to Italy was tolerable, but I had trouble getting comfortable in my seat. The young boy sitting next to me constantly shifted in his seat and jabbed me several times with his elbow while I tried to sleep. But the good news is, contrary to what I had feared, I made it through the flight without pain in my body or brain.

Once on the ground, I found my luggage and my driver and made it safely to the hotel. I spent the rest of the day relaxing before having to attend my first meeting the next day. Right next to the hotel in Vimercate was a mall with shops and a food court. I decided to venture out and check out the stores and also find a place to eat. This might appear to be a simple and normal task; however, for someone who previously needed assistance to venture out in her own hometown with a brain injury, I was about to set out on something even greater—a new place where I didn't even speak the language.

I found a place to eat and ordered a slice of pizza as it was the only thing I could understand on the menu, which was, of course, written in Italian. Lucky for me I could see the pizza slices right in front of me. What a strange experience being in a foreign country and not knowing the language. Afterward, I walked around for a while and then headed back to the hotel to rest a bit and watch some TV. Unfortunately all the TV stations, except one news station, were in Italian.

The next morning I met with a coworker whom I had only known through e-mail and conference calls. She was great, showing me where to get breakfast and pointing out all the good stuff like croissants that melt in your mouth. She escorted me to the office, which was within walking distance. How refreshing it was to walk to and from the office each day. I spent two weeks in Italy and gained even more confidence in my work ability as well as meeting great coworkers I had previously only known through telephone conversations.

This trip also gave me an opportunity to spend one weekend in Italy and sightsee. We were close to Milan, a popular city and tourist attraction; however, that weekend, it was the host for one of the biggest auto races—the Formula 1 Grand Prix race. This meant I needed to check out of my hotel and find another place to stay for the weekend.

My first instinct was to go into panic mode again, but quickly realized what a great opportunity to check out other cities such as Florence, Venice, and even Rome! My options were without limits. I chose to hop a train and set out to visit Venice. How many people in the Unites States can say, "I went to Venice for the weekend"? I was now one of those people. I think it is funny—going from someone who shivered at the thought of traveling to Italy to now planning to hop a train in a foreign country and head to another destination. If the truth be known, I really wasn't brave enough to do it alone.

Only God can orchestrate having a coworker from New Jersey who happened to be in Italy at the same time and agreed to travel with me to Venice. This took care of my lack of bravery. We took a limo from the office to the train station, staring up at Italian signs and hoping we were getting on the correct train. The train took us directly to Venice. We jumped on a water taxi taking us to the other side of Venice, and from the water taxi we made our way to the bus station for the final vehicle to take us to the hotel. Well, not quite—the bus proved to be the biggest challenge. We had to try to figure out which bus to take and when to let the driver know to stop. We did okay, but ended up walking for a mile or so before finally finding our hotel at around 11:00 p.m. We must have looked funny dragging our suitcases along the waterway in the dark in search of our hotel. But what a great experience for me to be able to get from one location to another in Italy, not even knowing the language. And this was only a couple of years after living with a brain injury where I was unable to understand people speaking in English or had the physical stamina to travel. Just doing one of these activities in the past would have completely wiped me out for days, now hopping from one vehicle to another with no limitations or aftereffects.

Our Venice weekend turned out to be wonderful. Our hotel gave us a free pass to visit Murano island where they produce Venetian glass. We were given a private tour of the factory and viewed a glass blowing exhibition, ending at a store to purchase souvenirs. While we shopped around, a young woman tried several times to get my attention. I wasn't really interested in being interrupted but finally decided to turn my attention to her since she was insistent. As we chatted, she shared how she and her husband had been saving for this trip for some time and just finished visiting Rome. She explained this was the trip of a lifetime for them to see the Pope and the Vatican. With excitement on her face, she emphasized how I had to find a way to get there. She persisted, "The Vatican is a must-see!" I mentioned I was on a business trip and wouldn't be able to get to Rome this time. Her disappointment was evident. I think we both assumed each other to be a Christian. For me, it was because she wanted to see the Pope and the Vatican, and she saw I wore a cross necklace.

When she kept insisting I said, "I don't really need to see the Vatican because I feel like I'm already walking in the footsteps of Paul." She widened her eyes, trying to understand what I meant, and stared at me.

"I believe Paul, the Apostle," I continued, "must have made his way through all of Italy as he was the one to bring the Gospel to the non-Jewish Gentiles." I further shared, "For me, because of Paul, I feel connected to the Bible days and don't need to go to the Vatican to feel the relationship to my Christian faith."

Well, I think I blew her mind; you could see the wheels in her head turning. We ended up chatting for over an hour while my coworker shopped in the gift store. This young lady had endless questions and wondered where I got all my information. I told her, "From the Bible." She had no idea all of this history and information about Jesus and the Apostles were contained in the Bible.

I also had an opportunity to share my testimony on healing and the miracle God did in my life. This young couple was so excited by our chance meeting—or was it a chance meeting? God placed me in Venice, Italy, at the same time this young couple from Connecticut traveled there? What an incredible experience to be able to share what I've learned about Jesus and help a young couple who were searching for God and to help them understand Him personally. Returning home from this trip, I shared with friends and coworkers how I received a free trip to Italy and all I had to do was spend time in a gift shop sharing my healing testimony and what I knew about God. How great He is!!!

I know if I hadn't agreed to this trip because of fear or not feeling ready, I would have missed this awesome experience. God equipped my brain and enabled me with the ability to process work information and have the strength to travel and the courage to venture out on my own in a foreign country. And all I had to do was be obedient and listen to His direction, and I enjoyed an experience in Italy with God using me to impact the lives of this young couple. It was an enablement God would use for me to travel and experience another trip of a lifetime. He showed me there wasn't anything I couldn't do now. I could process new information, travel and live in mainstream society, foreign or otherwise, without any limitations.

This trip gave me the confidence to step out in faith and showed me how much my physical stamina had increased. The whole experience left me feeling like I was on top of the world again.

I couldn't have been more wrong.

CHAPTER 9

You've Got to Be Kidding!

You will never believe what happened next. It was not one I expected. My new journey involved fear, something I had forgotten I had because of my faith and spiritual and emotional challenges where I felt all the ground I had previously gained was about to go down the drain.

The last Tuesday in February 2013 started out like any other day; however, it ended very differently. While driving to the office, stopped at a red light waiting to make a right-hand turn, a car driven by a pregnant woman struck my car from behind, evidently expecting my car had already proceeded through the right-hand turn. At the moment of impact, I thought, *You've got to be kidding me.* It was déjà vu all over again.

This was now the fourth time in my driving career my car had been struck and totaled while I had been at a complete stop. Why did people keep hitting my car, especially when at a full stop?

When someone hits you, there is normally a long pause and feeling like this really isn't happening. Then you come back to reality and recognize the questions you need to ask. Is anyone hurt? How much damage? Call the police and others.

Lucky for both of us, we appeared to be okay, and my first thought went to her since she was visibly pregnant and I learned she was six months along. The damage to my car on the surface didn't look so bad. However, I've been down this road before where something looked perfectly fine and ended up taking a different twist.

I immediately went into action by calling 911 to report the accident and then gathering up all the necessary information. The pregnant woman didn't think we needed to call the police; however, having been trained by my dad, a former police officer, I could hear him in my head saying: "First thing to do when you are in an accident is to call the police."

I pulled out my registration, insurance card, and driver's license and readied myself for when the police showed up. The woman forgot her cell phone and needed to use mine, didn't have her insurance card, and appeared totally unprepared. I tried to exchange information, but she didn't think we needed to, so I waited for the police to handle all the details.

The police arrived and asked the standard questions. My explanation showed me to be clearly in the right since I had been at a complete stop at the traffic light. The road I planned on turning right on was a busy four-lane highway, and my head had been turned to the left to ensure it was safe to proceed. Just as I was ready to make the turn was when the incredible jolt came in the rear. The driver behind me had fully accelerated into the back bumper of my car. At first glance, my car looked like only the right backlight, the entire right side of the car, and the back hutch had been crushed, but we would learn later more internal damage had occurred than I realized.

By now the police were writing up the report, and the woman's husband had shown up with her insurance card. We exchanged the necessary information. He seemed really nice and showed his concern about me.

"Are you okay?" he asked.

"Yes," I assured him. "I'm fine. But you really need to get your wife checked out, or at least call her doctor. After all, she's six months pregnant."

Funny, how quick we are to give other people advice and not take it for ourselves. For some reason, I always believe I'm indestructible and, as always, quickly learn it is not always the case.

I finished all the paperwork with the police and drove on to the office. Being a little late, I only missed my first meeting. Earlier, I already knew the day was going to be a long one. Meetings had been scheduled from morning until quitting time. Slightly unnerved from the accident and having a headache from the impact of being hit, I didn't feel like seeing or talking to anyone, so I kept my office door shut and joined the conference by phone which is typical these days. Staying isolated for eight hours should have been a clue I wasn't feeling myself since normally I love people, welcome interruptions, and enjoy talking with coworkers.

I didn't tell anyone I had been in a car accident; however, as the hours advanced the headache wasn't going away. While on a call with my boss, I shared what happened. We have a close relationship and were friends before she became my boss.

"Donna, you need to get checked out. You went through a previous concussion and traumatic brain injury, and I'd feel much better if you saw a doctor."

I tried to convince her I was fine, but deep down I too sensed something wasn't right.

I left a little early and drove to the Urgent Care Center close to the office. I'd been at this facility before and thought it a good idea to get instant attention rather than driving to my medical doctor. This place also had my previous CAT scans, and it just made sense to me. I'm so glad I did, as the doctor's initial tests and routine examination of asking me to walk a straight line, answer simple routine questions, and check my eyes determined a severe concussion. When trying to put one foot in front of the other, I ended up falling right over; and when the doctor asked my name and a few other easy questions, I hesitated after each question. I knew my name, but sometimes with a head injury or concussion, the processing of the answer takes time resulting in a delay to respond. I had been down this road before and instantly knew this wasn't good. Sitting on the emergency table, I wished it to be a dream. How could it be happening again?

The doctor ordered a CAT scan, and as I lay inside the machine, my thoughts quickly turned to disbelief. *How could this be happening to me again*? It didn't seem real, but it was real. I was reexperiencing the all too familiar symptoms again—the ones I had lived with for 13 ½ years. I tried so hard to keep my emotions in check, all the while wanting to burst into tears.

While waiting for the results to confirm the doctor's diagnosis of a concussion, I started to talk to Jesus, "Lord, I know you healed me before, so this time shouldn't be any different." Even though I could see and feel the familiar symptoms, I knew deep down they had to leave again, just like they did a couple of years ago when God dramatically healed me of my brain injury.

I sat in the hospital room alone and kept hearing the doctor's words echoing in my head, "You have a severe concussion." Reflecting back, I realized this amounted to my fifth concussion. This was incredible! How could I have had five concussions, all except one, from car accidents? I want to be clear and get this point across—*none* of the car accidents were my fault, and all were from someone hitting me while I was totally stopped. The one exception had been the accident where I had skidded on black ice. It didn't seem real or make any sense.

I left the Urgent Care Center and drove myself home. I know you are thinking, *How does someone with a concussion drive home?* I still don't know, but the doctor's instructions were no TV, no computer, rest, and no brain activity. He never said anything about driving. I wonder if he even knew I had driven myself to the hospital. Since no one told me not to drive, I just naturally drove home without giving it another thought. With concussions (which is a brain injury), there isn't a lot of rationalization, and you end up just doing what comes naturally or what someone tells you to do. All I knew was I wanted to be home in my house, and the only way to get there was to drive my car. Lucky for me, I was only about fifteen minutes away and a straight route to get there.

Once I arrived home, I sent a text to my friend Elisa so she knew I wouldn't be in the office the next day. I also wanted her to agree with me in prayer that these symptoms had to vanish. The final report from the doctor showed a severe concussion, but the only report I wanted to focus on was the one that would come from Jesus. I knew He could take away my pain and the familiar symptoms and completely heal my brain.

I know my instructions from the doctor were no texting, but how do you stop 100 percent texting when you need to inform people? Elisa called our friend Cathy, whom God had put in my life to teach me about healing and was instrumental in my healing journey with the brain injury. I knew I was in good hands with God. And you can't get any better than having prayer warriors like Elisa and Cathy. I knew it was only a matter of time when these new symptoms had to leave. However, having lived with these types before, it was really hard and emotionally upsetting to have them back again. I'm sure Elisa could feel my emotion through the phone, and she recorded a video of her seven-year-old son praying for my healing. How precious are the prayers of a child! I knew God heard and honored them. This little boy's prayers sustained me through my testing experience.

The days and weeks were challenging. I tried to walk as a healed person; however, the symptoms were difficult and getting worse. My slow, awkward, and off-balance walking tipped me over many times. Trying to turn everything off in your life for a period of time, no TV, computer, reading, music, texting, and puzzles, nothing to stimulate your brain, seemed almost impossible. I had to find quiet, simple TV shows to have on so I could listen but not watch them. Most of the days my eyes needed to remain closed which ended up with me falling asleep. Sleep is actually good for the brain to heal.

My vision and focus was slightly impaired, and my eyes experienced pain, so I couldn't read my Bible. Therefore, I used the TV and CDs of Christian music and Christian teachings on DVDs to ensure God's Word surrounded me during this time. My friend Jeannette mentioned to me that I should laugh during this time. Laughing would keep me focused that the pain and symptoms had to leave. God reminded me about a Christian comedian I had seen the previous year. Jeannette helped me find his web site, and I listened to video clips on this web site. God brought back to remembrance laughing so hard I couldn't breathe the previous year. This helped me during my recovery. I love that while my brain wasn't functioning correctly, God enabled me to remember this comedian's name.

About three weeks into this latest journey, the pain in my eyes and head became excruciating. Jeannette called me, saying she felt something was wrong. I have a habit of not telling anyone when I'm struggling, but God has a habit of letting my friends know. "Thank you God for always telling on me." ☺

I shared with Jeannette about my eyes being really bad and whenever I moved the pain increased. She told me, "Keep your eyes focused on Jesus." Afterward, I laid down and kept repeating, "My eyes are focused on you Jesus." I woke up the next day without the intense pain in my head and eyes.

Prior to Jeannette's call, my pastor had also called to check on me. He had been at the hospital as his mother was very ill. God had placed on his heart to call me, and I was overwhelmed at God's love for me, also for my pastor who took time to call me while his family struggled with their own family issues. He shared with me something that was a key to unlocking my next healing.

Several times during our conversation, he said the following:

"Donna, this is not the same as last time."

I didn't really process or understand what he meant, but in a couple of days it was revealed to me. I thanked him for his time and caring about me. He prayed with me, and his prayer encompassed agreeing with me in my healing. I had grown so much in these five years knowing healing prayers were released for me. Now, my pastor and others were once again agreeing with me for the manifestation of the proof. Relying on others' prayers might sound subtle or inconsequential to others, but to me it was powerful as they recognized my faith growth as a result. I didn't need to beg God to heal me, as I knew it had already taken place. So, patiently in faith, I waited for the symptoms to leave.

Three weeks after the car accident and the morning after Jeanette's phone call, I was listening to Joyce Meyer on TV. It was 11:40 a.m. when I heard her say, "Call out to Jesus." It felt like a command, and I immediately stopped dead in my tracks. There, in the middle of the living room floor, I called Jesus's name three times. It was as simple as "Jesus, Jesus, Jesus." Instantly something started from the top of my head and down to the floor like something was falling off me. At first, I thought my clothes had dropped off to the floor. My instinct was to squat down and reach out my hands to catch what had fallen. Within seconds, I stood up and realized my brain was wide awake again, and the pain in my head and eyes had vanished. I knew that I knew I was completely healed again!!!

I walked right over to the dining room table without missing a beat and began working on my computer, feeling like I replicated the story in the Bible about Peter's mother-in-law. She had a fever, and Jesus commanded the fever to leave, and she got up and started fixing a meal as if nothing had happened. How great is our God! The next day my eyes were fully restored to the point I could work from home and complete a detailed excel spreadsheet that would have been impossible the day before—not only be able to actually see the document but complete all the required actions.

With my brain fully operational again, I wanted to understand why it took three weeks for the manifestation of my healing and the experience of what fell off me. I spent time with God and thanked Him for my healing, and in answer to my first question, He revealed to me it was fear that had fallen off.

Hmmm, fear? What was that all about? Typically, I didn't consider myself a fearful person. Well, I guess I thought I wasn't. Fear comes in all shapes and sizes, sometimes unrecognizable to us. I had believed the words I spoke during these three weeks and felt they were positive and full of faith; however, in actuality, there must have been some fear in my words from unconsciously making a connection to my previous brain injury I had lived with for 13 ½ years. For example, when I got dizzy or experienced pain and symptoms, I said to myself and others, "That's okay; I've experienced these symptoms before."

While my intentions were good and I thought I hadn't given in to the symptoms or linking them to my past brain injury, I believed deep down inside of me as the symptoms dragged on, I must have unconsciously been feeling *What if these symptoms don't go away?* That's called "unbelief." Giving in to the symptoms opened the door to fear in my life and blocked the ability to walk as a healed and whole person.

Reflecting back on this three-week journey, I realized my thoughts and words weren't strong and authoritative. I never "commanded" the symptoms to leave my body. It continues to amaze me how powerful our words in our lives are, either for positive or negative results. While I thought my words were positive and believed I had total faith in God to heal and restore my body, my deep down emotions, however, must have conveyed something different.

I can't say I enjoyed the healing process; however, the blessings of meeting Jesus in my living room and the instant feeling of healing over my body when everything dropped off was an indescribable experience. What was the biggest blessing from this experience? During this time, I was able to show nonbelievers how to walk in God's grace and to faithfully deal with symptoms and challenges until they are removed and share another incredible experience of healing, showing God is still in the miracle business.

The saddest outcome of this accident happened to my car. It had been declared totaled, and now I had to go car shopping. The exterior of the car didn't appear to be in too bad of shape; however, the insurance adjuster indicated the damage had been too severe and costly to repair it. My heart was crushed when they towed my car away. This car and I had been through so many journeys together: God spoke to me daily in this car. The manifestation of my healing from the initial 13 ½-year brain injury took place in this car. God revealed many revelations, including seeing my giant rainbow, in this car; and I obtained victories and challenges in overcoming, by getting in this car and driving.

I did not want to let this car go, but had to realize the miracles and experiences lived inside of me and not the car. Nevertheless, God showed me that part of the fear that was trying to grip me was being without a car. At the same time feeling the need to get a car even though I wasn't able to drive was crazy thinking. Unfortunately, that is how an injured brain thinks. When your brain is injured, your thinking is dramatically affected.

A friend drove me to different car dealerships; and, as only God can orchestrate, I was able to share my healing journey with several of the salesmen. Once totally healed from this recent healing miracle, meaning all my symptoms as well as my fear, I was able to share how Jesus healed my brain again!

These kinds of journeys are challenging, but also rewarding. It is an awesome feeling of being blessed. I'm honored that God has equipped me for these journeys, and I love being able to share them with others, especially you the readers who may be dealing with a traumatic brain injury or other symptoms and challenges.

I did purchase a new car, and I was getting used to a larger one with lots of gadgets. Friends encouraged me to purchase a bigger one to keep me safe and I'm believing for great conversations with God in this car as well. We have also asked God for a *huge* hedge of protection around this vehicle with no more accidents!

Now, fully healed with another incredible testimony and a car packed with a navigational system, I anticipated future journeys would all be safe ones.

So where would God send me next?

CHAPTER 10

Being Sent Out

My first reaction to a friend's suggestion about a trip to Israel was "No way!" Instantly my thoughts went to all the reasons it would be impossible for me to take this type of trip. The plane ride was too far, my health wasn't perfect, and terrorists were shooting missiles at Israel. While I had been healed of the latest brain injury (concussion), I had not fully regained the physical endurance I felt I needed for such a trip, and the suggestion came only months after this latest healing.

For a couple of years, I listened to my friend share her desire to go to Israel. I countered it each time with the suggestion: "Let's go to Florida where there is a park designed as an exact replica of Israel." My thinking was: *It's much closer and safer and can give us the same type of experience.* Well, I couldn't have been more wrong.

The summer of 2013 my friend's church advertised an upcoming trip in eight months to Israel. The cost appeared extremely reasonable, and it looked like the perfect trip. My heart longed to walk in the footsteps of Jesus and see the Bible come alive, although anxiety gripped me about the possible dangers and whether I would be physically able to travel. I decided to pray about traveling and felt God put it on my heart to go. Really? How could God even consider my physical body and brain were ready for a long plane ride to Israel? It wasn't even a year since my last brain injury. Further, I heard all the stories about violence caused by local extremists and the region being attacked. My mind and heart were conflicted, "Isn't it dangerous traveling to Israel?"

Normally, I am a determined person. I face my fears and drive forward toward something even if it scares me. So, believing God wanted me to go, I agreed to press forward and nevertheless continued to have doubts. I declared to God: "If I am not physically able to go on this trip or if it is too dangerous, please cancel it." I sat back, believed, and put my trust in Him.

The weeks and months crept by with no indication of the trip being canceled, so I started to prepare myself mentally and emotionally. "Was I actually going to do this, get on a plane, and travel six thousand miles across the Atlantic Ocean to Israel?" I casually mentioned my Israel trip to a couple of friends to see their reaction, hoping they would strengthen my confidence about taking this trip. They did, and I finally gained my needed confidence and *knew* I needed to go. When I get these feelings of knowing, I can't explain them, they just come, but I've learned something magical usually happens. In this instance, the detailed, planning part of my brain kicked in and took over turning my focus to preparation, what to wear, what to bring, and what to see. One item on my list was to locate the one area in Israel I needed to see—the place where the woman with the blood issue touched Jesus's hem. I searched the Bible and the internet and e-mailed pastors I knew to see if anyone could tell me about the exact spot. The only clue I found was the spot could be found in Capernaum, located in the northern part of Israel. How exciting, we were going to be in that locale the first part of our trip! Somehow, I knew within my heart we would be near the spot. I was now ready for my trip to Israel.

Arriving at the airport, I looked for opportunities and open doors to share my love for God and tell about the incredible miracles He had done in my life. My first opportunity came while standing in line for security and baggage check. I met two older couples traveling together from Florida who were also on their way to Israel for the first time. We chatted, and then the opening occurred as only God can orchestrate. I'm never sure how it happens, but He somehow provided an opening, and I found myself sharing my testimony about being healed of a traumatic brain injury and what an incredible miracle trip for me to journey to God's promised land. They were amazed and thrilled to learn God's miracles still happen today.

We passed through the first security checkpoint with little difficulty. However, I had locked my suitcase, which I always do, but much to the dismay of security. So I was asked additional questions to ensure I had not packed a bomb. When the security guy mentioned this to me, I kind of thought he was kidding but then took him seriously knowing this trip to Israel was different and so was the security, so I stayed focused on answering his questions correctly. I felt totally safe as I watched the security agents do their job and didn't mind the extra questioning or being asked to unlock my suitcase.

My friend's church was the sponsor of this trip, so she knew several of the people joining us on this trip. It was exciting getting to know new Christians even before boarding the plane. I couldn't believe how ready I was for this new adventure. All my previous concerns and worries were a distant memory as I waited to board the plane taking me to the land where Jesus walked—the promised land.

The plane ride was about eleven hours, but the excitement of looking forward to stepping on God's land made the trip seemed quick. We ate, watched some TV, read, talked, stretched our legs, and then slept. We were advised to try to sleep because the moment our feet hit land, we would be off and touring our first stop. What a shock to my body as we got off the plane. We left Newark Airport with winter coats and landed in Tel Aviv to a temperature in the high '90s.

While heading to our first stop on the tour bus, my mind raced realizing I would be standing out in the desert sun. I left my suntan lotion and hat packed in my luggage and not my carry-on bag. Lucky for me, the jacket I wore on the plane had a hood, and I could use it to cover my head and face to avoid sunburn and heat exhaustion.

Before taking this trip, everyone I met who had been to Israel before said, "This will be a trip of a lifetime, and the Bible will 'come alive' for you." While I totally believed everyone, you can't imagine how the experience of visiting the Holy Land truly proved to be just that. The Bible really does "come alive." You actually have to experience it to understand what that really means.

After the first three days, with another week left, we had already seen and experienced so much that I couldn't even imagine there could be more to see of this great country. During the first part of our vacation, we stayed at the Sea of Galilee in the northern part of Israel. This area is the most peaceful place I have ever experienced. We had our own little kibbutz, which was absolutely adorable and overlooked the Sea of Galilee with an incredible view. A kibbutz is a communal farm-like settlement in Israel. Each night after returning from sightseeing and eating dinner, we would meet at the Sea and worship God. What an absolutely amazing way to end each day and prepare us for a restful sleep. Many times during these evenings, my body felt like it was floating, and I realized this is what total relaxation feels like—something I never typically experienced, being a type A personality and always actively in control of everything.

On the third day of our trip, we made it to Capernaum. Standing outside the synagogue where Jesus entered on the Sabbath and stood up to read from the scroll of Isaiah, I finally mustered enough nerve to ask our tour guide a question.

"Can you tell me where Mark 5:34 occurred, where Jesus said to the women with the issue of blood, 'Daughter, your faith has made you well?'"

"No one knows the exact spot," he replied, "but it happened in this general area."

He then gave me a puzzled look and asked, "Why do you want to know the exact spot?" I gathered no one had ever asked this specific question. I shared how much this scripture had meant to me while living with a brain injury and how each day I waited to hear those exact words from God, "Daughter, your faith has made you well." I continued to share how I was radically healed by God. The tour guide stood in complete amazement at my story. When I finished sharing, I realized a crowd of people had gathered around us listening to my healing testimony.

Back on the bus, the tour guide asked the pastor if he had heard my testimony, and the pastor revealed he had and then quickly looked at me and said: "You need to share your story." My response: "I just did." He then repeated with a smile, "You need to share your testimony." I then knew what he meant, to share my testimony with the rest of the group.

Later in the evening, while dressing for dinner and recounting my incredible experience of testifying to the tour guide and those who listened, I felt God put into my heart that I had shared my story at the same spot where Jesus stood reading the scriptures pertaining to Himself (Luke 4:17). I sunk to my knees at the thought I had actually stood in His footsteps and was able to share my precious journey about how He had touched my life and changed it forever.

Before going to bed and reflecting on the day, I prayed and felt a gentle push from God to make myself available to share my testimony if another opportunity arose. I've always been ready to tell my story, but have been shy and sensitive about sharing before large groups, unless someone in an authoritative position asks me. Normally, I'm more comfortable sharing in a one-on-one situation. Through the night I told God, "If the pastor happens to be sitting alone at breakfast, I will let him know I'm available."

Of course, the next morning I found the pastor sitting alone and knew I needed to be obedient and inform him about my conversation through the night with God. Pastor immediately smiled and told me there would definitely be an opportunity for me to share. I asked God to find the perfect place and moment for me, and He absolutely delivered

I knew on the trip they would offer a water baptism, and I prayed about it since I had already been water baptized. I loved the idea of simulating water baptism in the Jordan River where Jesus had been baptized. I felt it would be a once in a lifetime experience. However, we learned the water area where Jesus had been baptized wasn't safe and several people had become sick. Our trip leaders decided they weren't about to take a chance and chose a park they knew along the tour route. Since I had wanted the Jordan experience, I planned not to participate. But as only God can orchestrate, the baptism somehow was moved from the park to the Sea of Galilee.

When I heard this, how could I not participate? I felt the Sea could be the perfect place.

Standing at the edge of the water waiting for our ceremony to begin, my emotions were so completely overwhelming I could barely breathe. My mind raced from picturing myself disabled and sitting on the sofa staring out the window to now standing with my feet in the Sea of Galilee waiting to be water baptized—and only a short distance away from the Jordan River where Jesus performed the same routine! Tears streamed down my face while others looked at me not understanding my emotions. Only a few people knew of my healing journey, so they probably thought this might be my first time being baptized. Because of my emotions and I was scarcely able to speak, people would not learn about my healing story until later.

Just as the sun started to set in the background, my turn finally came. I walked into the water out to where the pastors stood, and the moment was absolutely perfect. Pastor asked me if I had been baptized, and before responding I realized I was being baptized differently, this time as a healed and whole person. My previous baptism was special, but it was during the time I lived with the brain injury. This moment was even more special as I walked into the water to rededicate my life to my Lord and Savior.

On our last night at the Sea of Galilee, we sat by the Sea worshipping God. The sky was dark except for some twinkling stars and the city lights on the hill across the Sea. I heard the pastor asking for volunteers to share about anything on their hearts. Everything was completely still and even more silent since no one had spoken up. Then, I heard a familiar voice behind me calling out my name and asking me to share my story. My heart raced at the thought of getting up and speaking in front of everyone, but once I started talking about my God and what He had done in my life, a peace and calmness engulfed me and I let God's words pour out of me. This was my first time speaking outside in the dark of night and even more precious at the Sea of Galilee where Jesus performed 70 percent of His miracles. Words can't express my emotion at that time, even to this day, of the special gift I had been given to stand in the footsteps of Jesus and how proud and blessed I felt to share the miracle He performed in my life. God had indeed chosen the perfect moment and the perfect place for me to share my story.

While I have dozens of special memories and stories of my trip to Israel, standing in the Sea of Galilee was the defining moment in my life. When my body went down into the Sea, I felt it put an end to the chapter of my life about sickness and symptoms.

Rising out of the water, I would now begin the next chapter in my journey and the work God has called me to do, sharing my testimony on healing.

CHAPTER 11

Victories That Build Faith Muscles

How does one go about sharing their testimony and boldly stepping out to what God has called you to do? By first going through stuff!

In this book, I've been sharing my journey over the last several years; however, to truly get the whole picture, we need to journey back in time to experiences I encountered over the course of my life.

We all have stories or experiences in life that might be considered little God miracles enabling us to build our faith muscles and strengthening our trust in God for the new challenges we face in life.

Here are a few of those stories that helped build my faith muscles enabling me to completely trust in God when I faced the bigger challenges.

Jessie's Cross

I will never forget one special July 4, 1996, when my youngest goddaughter, Jessie, was about three years old. We always celebrated Independence Day together with a home picnic and later seeing the fireworks at a local park. She loved playing with the cross necklace and Bible pendant I wore around my neck given to me by both my grandmothers.

We had just finished our picnic, and Jessie was sitting on my lap opening my Bible pendant and asking me to read the inscription. Inside this tiny Bible pendant was the Lord's Prayer. Thank goodness I knew it by heart. The tiny print was almost impossible to read. As she held the Bible and little cross in her hands, I mentioned to her that she also had a cross she could wear when she got older, but presently was with her mom for safe keeping.

I had bought Jessie the cross for her baby baptism, and it filled me with joy when she wore it the day I held her at the church altar and dedicated her to God. Of course Jessie only focused on the fact she had a cross necklace and pestered me to let her wear it. *What harm could it do*, I thought, *as long as she was in the house?* So I went and got it. (Mothers, I know, are already ahead of my story. She wasn't going to take the cross necklace off when we left the house.)

Preparing to leave for the fireworks, we tried to get Jessie to take off the necklace. Unfortunately, we were unsuccessful, and she kept it around her neck as we walked to the park. *What if it falls off and she loses it?* My thoughts swirled. Sitting on the grass in my beach chair I watched her run around, my eyes never leaving her neck or the necklace. I am a very sentimental person and wanted to ensure she didn't lose it so she would have it as she grew up, just like I had my cross necklace and Bible locket given to me by my grandmothers.

Of course, the next time I looked at Jessie's neck, I saw the chain but the cross was missing. I thought, *Don't panic and don't say anything to Jessie. She'll only be upset.* I motioned to my friend that the cross was missing. By this time, dusk had rolled in, and I thought the cross would be impossible to find in the grass.

We quietly started to look so as not to get Jessie upset, when it hit me. God knew exactly where the cross was. I closed my eyes and prayed. God knew how important this cross necklace was to me and how I wanted Jessie to have it as she grew up. I prayed for Him to reveal where it was. When I opened my eyes, the cross appeared on the tip of my sneaker. I had been sitting in my chair with my feet in front of me all this time, and there was no way the cross was there before praying. God had to have laid her cross there. What a miracle and awesome experience! These are the type of miracles you hold on to. They enable you to build faith muscles for the future.

God truly does answer prayers, and this is an example of a teaching moment and the start of my faith muscles being strengthened, as well as the beginning of an incredible journey with God.

Learning How to Pray

My grandmother had always been the light of my world. She lived with me my entire life, and we even shared an apartment together, when it was time to move out on my own. Many times as a child and young teenager, my Gram and I walked to church together. It felt even more significant due to the special connection and bond we had about God being the center of both our lives. Then in July 1999, she fell and broke her hip. It proved to be a serious injury for a woman of her age. She spent time in the hospital and eventually moved to a rehabilitation center.

Gram reached a beautiful age of 87, and the fall and hospitalization started to reveal her frailty. It broke my heart to see her failing. I prayed earnestly to God to heal her and restore her to total health but felt my prayers were not being heard. During this time in my life, I didn't really understand God as a Father or Healer. I only knew God intellectually, although still believing He was involved in this situation with me and Gram.

From July to November, I spent most of the time driving to the rehab place to visit her. This really drained me as I still had the brain injury and any physical or emotional activity exhausted me causing pressure and pain in both my brain and body. However, I never wanted to give up on the time I could spend with her. I didn't want to look back on my life and have any regrets. During our visits, we talked about life and what she meant to me in my years growing up. We spent time sharing stories, reminiscing about the past, and looking forward to the future and the pending birth of my niece and her great-granddaughter.

With Thanksgiving approaching, Gram had grown weak and tired. Each morning during my time with God, I cried out to Him. I couldn't bear the thought of her leaving and no longer being in my life. One morning while crying out to God, I felt God showed me my prayers were selfish in wanting to hold on to her. God revealed to me how to pray for *His* will for her life, not what was best for *my* life.

While I prayed for God's grace and His peace and will for her life, I felt God's comforting arms wrap around me. He gave me strength to let go of my grandmother and give her life back to Him. I had an incredible peace and strength I can't begin to describe. Praying God's will was an entirely new way to pray. A couple of days after Thanksgiving, and after her three grandchildren and her great-grandson were able to see her and say goodbye, Gram went home to be with the Lord. After her passing I couldn't even speak. I was so lost and felt alone. She was my rock.

While devastated at the loss, God gave me the strength and ability to give her eulogy. Never in my wildest dreams could I have imagined me standing in front of relatives in a church and doing this. When meeting with the local minister and sharing stories about my Gram, the minister thought I would be perfect to speak at the service for her. My immediate reaction was "No way." Even my mother said, "No, we don't do that." In most funeral services we had attended, the minister would say a few words, and then you went to the burial site where the minister spoke again.

The night before my grandmother's funeral service, I felt God tugging on my heart to speak at her service. I told God, "If I am going to do this, you are going to have to give me the words because I have no idea what to say." Further, of course, I reminded Him how uncomfortable I was with public speaking, more especially at a funeral service in front of family and friends.

The morning before the service, I got up, and God's Words came flowing out of me. I quickly grabbed a pen and paper and started writing the thoughts flowing from my head. Amazingly, I never really agreed to speak. I wasn't sure how the minister knew to call on me; but, at one point in the service, the minister announced, "Donna will speak on behalf of the family." You could have heard a pin drop as I'm sure my family and friends were shocked at the thought of me standing up in front of people and speaking because I was so distraught at the loss of my Gram. Come to think about it. I don't think anyone in my family ever heard me speak aloud, especially not in public.

I will never forget that moment when I spoke about my Gram and was able to share what a truly amazing and extraordinary person she was. I spoke in the same church where she and I had worshipped together, and that experience began a new journey in my life of sharing and testifying.

Shortly after her passing, I was asked to speak at other churches, this time sharing my brain injury journey and eventually my healing testimony.

It is amazing how God gives us different moments to listen to His promptings, and each of these moments add up and contributes to strengthening our faith muscles. I know in my heart standing up in church the day I eulogized my grandmother began an incredible journey. If I had not taken advantage of that opportunity, I might have missed God's blessing and his eventual call on my life.

A Chance Encounter

During the early years of my brain injury journey, I had been unable to attend church on a weekly basis. It had been difficult to be in large crowds and be exposed to loud noises. Even sitting in an upright position for a long period of time caused pain, confusion, and total exhaustion. I chose to stay at home versus attempting to drive to church and put my brain and body through those challenges. Having been someone who loves going to church every Sunday, I found another way to hear God's Word being preached, through television. I'm not sure how, but all of a sudden Dr. Charles Stanley appeared on my TV each Sunday morning. This became my routine every week, sitting on the sofa with a pen and paper trying to capture his messages. His style and format were perfect for me during this time. I even continue today to tune in on Sunday mornings.

A couple of years after I sustained my brain injury, I learned Dr. Stanley would be visiting Ocean Grove, New Jersey, which is only an hour away from where I lived. I knew I had to go to this event and meet the man God put in my life during this difficult time—but how to find a way to get me there? This, of course, left all the pressure on my friend. Much of my memory of this event is foggy. I don't remember the date, the year, the message, or even if we stayed overnight, but I do remember one life-changing encounter with Dr. Stanley.

The story in the Bible I have identified with the most is the woman who had an issue with blood for twelve years and who did everything she could to touch the hem of Jesus knowing she would be healed. I completely identified with this story on so many levels and knew I needed to "touch" Dr. Stanley. My friend tried to reassure me even if we went to see Dr. Stanley speak, the chances were impossible to personally meet him. I'm not sure how I can explain the feeling, but I knew I would meet him and he would "touch" my life.

These types of events are held at the Great Auditorium in Ocean Grove and are free with no seat assignments. This leaves everyone on a mad dash to find seats. For most people, this isn't a big deal. The procedure is to wait in line and then make your way to find a seat. For my friend and me, the challenge was finding a place somewhere out of the way of the crowds and not in the sun, to sit and wait while she tried to keep one eye on me and stand in a long line in order to enter the building.

We arrived at the auditorium early enough, so we were close to the front of the line. My friend wanted to ensure we were near the stage to secure front row seats as I still experienced claustrophobic sensations. I couldn't handle people sitting on either side of me in close quarters, even squished with seats in front and back. I know I really was a handful in those days. I can only express how great our God was as we entered the auditorium. People were running for the front row seats and passing us by, whereby my pace was only .08 miles per hour. For you, non-number types, it is equivalent to a shuffle step.

When we made our way to the front, we found two seats off to the side but in the front row. We sat down and waited with great anticipation for Dr. Stanley to speak. I'm not sure I knew what I had been expecting, but I had a pull inside telling me I needed to touch him, even if it was the "hem" of his jacket.

My friend continued to remind me even though we were sitting close to the stage, Dr. Stanley would be on stage and I couldn't reach him from my seat. She explained it wasn't the same as in the Bible and Dr. Stanley wasn't Jesus, which of course I knew, but I felt a compelling urge to meet him face to face and "touch" him.

I can't recall anything he said or even spoke about, but at the end of his teaching he said he would come down off the stage and meet people—and, as only God can orchestrate, he chose the side of the stage where we were sitting.

I'm sure my friend panicked, realizing the rush of people down the aisles heading in our direction. How would she get me to where Dr. Stanley was standing and at the same time ensure I wouldn't be jostled by the crowds or lost in the shuffle? For me, I didn't have a worry or care in the world. I focused only on meeting the man whom God had placed in my life to lead me more deeply to the Lord and who had been speaking weekly into my life teaching me about Jesus. To me, Dr. Stanley was the closest thing to God during my isolating period of living with the brain injury. While I knew he wasn't God and didn't put him on the same pedestal, he was, however, a godly man and knew the Creator who would eventually heal my brain and body.

The moment finally came. I watched him walk toward the side of the stage and toward me. I rose from my seat and headed toward the railing. I have no idea if my friend was with me or even if she knew where I was. My eyes focused only on Dr. Stanley.

Within seconds of shaking his hand, an incredible surge went from his hand to mine and then through my entire body, almost like a charge of electrical current. It was an absolutely amazing experience and one I will never forget. Before this experience, my body and brain were usually lethargic and in a constant exhausted state; however, after shaking Dr. Stanley's hand, the surge of energy and alertness I experienced continued even after we left. Since I didn't have a complete understanding yet that God wanted me well, I feel this experience gave me a glimpse of the incredible miracles to come in the years ahead.

I continue to this day to recall the surge of energy I felt in meeting Dr. Stanley and believe God simulated for me the scripture verse I love so much when the women with the blood issue touched Jesus's garment and power went out from Him. While I didn't totally understand the experience at the time, I believe what I felt in my body when I shook his hand was the same type of power that came from Jesus to the woman with the issue of blood. As the days and weeks passed, my energy level increased, and I know my faith increased as well.

I truly believe I had an encounter with God who touched me through Dr. Stanley. These encounters with God not only touch your life but also increase your faith and provide you with mini victories to carry you through the more challenging times ahead.

Trusting God Again

Three months before I learned more about the healing power of God, my faith muscles were tested and exercised one more time. At the end of 2007 during a routine physical, my doctor felt a little lump near my thyroid. He didn't seem concerned but felt we should get it checked. All indications were a small cyst, which I've had in other places on my body and would require a simple aspiration to get rid of the fluid. Of course, when the aspiration is near your throat, it doesn't seem as simple as when in other parts of your body where the tissue is fatty and cushioning.

I went to a specialist, and they performed a biopsy on my throat. I have to say with all the other exams and tests I've been through over the years, having someone stick a needle in the middle of your throat isn't the greatest feeling and is pretty uncomfortable. I managed to get through it and thought the worst was over, or so I thought. The results came back indicating it was a rapidly growing mass. The only course of action was to have it surgically removed. Okay, those are words you don't want to hear: *You're going to have someone cut near your throat and vocal cords.* Unfortunately, to add complications, the doctors were concerned about putting me under anesthesia because of the brain injury. Just the thought of going into the hospital for surgery terrified me. I had never had major surgery, and I wasn't about to agree to this as I believed God could heal me. He simply wasn't going to put me through this huge surgery after living with a brain injury for twelve years.

I listened to what the doctors said and made the decision not to have the surgery. However, as the months progressed, so did the mass in my throat. I now had trouble breathing and swallowing. I set out to find a specialist who would help me find another option besides surgery. It was amazing how the doctors I met were oblivious to my brain injury and only concerned with removing the mass.

I asked this question to each doctor: "What can happen to me under anesthesia?" Their response was "You might not wake up, or you could lose the progress you've made cognitively." Wow, what options—choke to death, not wake up from surgery, or go backward in all the progress I'd made so far in developing and strengthening my brain.

Since I had to have the operation, I prepared myself for the possibility of not waking up or else dying. I'm not sure why my thoughts went in this direction, but I didn't have confidence about the surgery, *no* doubt from listening to the doctors' doom and gloom reports.

Prior to the surgery, I visited several churches and even called a local Christian radio station and asked questions about healing. My thinking: I believed God could heal me, and I wouldn't need the surgery. But at this time in my understanding on healing, I just wasn't sure He would do it for *me*. I didn't learn about healing scriptures until a year later. Each church I visited prayed with me, but no one believed 100 percent in my healing. So now I needed to prepare myself for the operation.

One day during lunch while sitting with a coworker, I asked him: "How do I say goodbye to the people in my life?" He reacted immediately to my question, almost yelling at me, "That is no way to prepare for an operation! How can you think like that?" I had been pretty much convinced my options were either not waking up or my cognitive deficit might be so bad I wouldn't remember people again. My coworker snapped me out of my negative thinking and must have jarred something inside of me. I quickly turned my attention to God to get me through this experience.

Funny how at times in our lives we reach out to God and He is the center of our thoughts and other times during a crisis we forget to call out to Him for help and guidance. I'm not sure if it was the prayers from the church people I had met in my search for healing or the radio DJ—or could it have been the Holy Spirit grabbing hold of my spirit? Whatever happened, my thinking changed dramatically. My confidence turned toward God with a belief in whatever happened during the surgery, He would be there with me and get me through any challenge. I had such a peace inside of me. It is hard to explain.

The day of the surgery, I was so relaxed they didn't even give me anything to knock me out before wheeling me into the operating room. My two friends and I were laughing and telling stories right up to the time the doctors came in for a pre-check. I had such faith. I was convinced God had already removed the mass. I told the surgeon before he operated to double-check since I knew God had removed it. I'm sure the doctor thought I was crazy, but I had total trust and faith in God for a miracle.

The surgery was successful, and the mass turned out to be noncancerous which was indeed a blessing. Strange, the idea of cancer wasn't even a thought of mine the entire time the doctors kept calling it a mass. When I first opened my eyes, I quickly started singing a song in my head to see if I remembered the words and I did. I believed I had all my cognitive thinking which later proved to be correct. There was no additional damage. Praise God. While in recovery, the surgeon mentioned they did have trouble with the breathing tube, and it had damaged my vocal cords. At this time, they weren't sure how permanent until the swelling left my throat area. I tried to speak but had no voice and trouble swallowing.

Unbelievable! I had just started to share my story about living as a brain injury survivor, and now the doctors were having me believe I might have lost my voice. No way, I knew my voice would not be taken away from me, but for more than a month, I had to trust God in the full restoration of it. Slowly, I regained my voice even though to me it sounded like the pitch was a little lower. But here's the great news: It came back and I am talking again!

During this challenging journey, I had to put my total trust and faith in the Lord. I had given Him my life and knew whatever the outcome of the surgery and my recovery, He would carry me through it. I believe this was a defining moment in my healing journey, as a year after this surgery was when I attended the women's conference I mentioned in Chapter 1 and where I met someone who taught me God was still in the miracle business today. I had definitely been a recipient of one of His miracles.

Another Challenging Experience

Just before experiencing my incredible healing miracle, I lived through another challenging experience five months after the thyroid surgery. While driving home from my goddaughter's thirteenth birthday celebration at a nearby restaurant, I was hit head-on by another driver who had lost control of her car.

While ascending up a curvy hill, I could see the car descending in the opposite direction, appearing out of control. I quickly reacted and steered my car to the side of the road and up against the guardrail and completely stopped hoping to get out of her way. I had no other options. Unfortunately, she still hit me head-on. If it hadn't been for the guardrail, my car would have been pushed over the edge down the side of the hill. Do you see a pattern here? Once again, my car was completely stopped, and someone hit me.

I ended up diagnosed with another concussion on top of my already existing brain injury and at a time when I had begun making tremendous progress with my cognitive and physical skills.

The front of my car was severely damaged and was being towed away. I needed someone to pick me up. I had just left my friend Linda and her family at the restaurant and lucky for me was able to reach them. My oldest goddaughter Lauren was in her twenties and immediately jumped into action. She came to get me and took me back to their house instead of my home. I wanted to go home, but she insisted, "Aunt Donna, we need to monitor you since you already have a brain injury. We want to make sure you are okay."

While at the time I thought she was overreacting, in reality she was exactly right. I'm so proud of her. She took control of the situation and knew exactly the right thing to do. I spent the night at their house, and my two goddaughters closely watched over me.

Linda drove me home the next day, and I called work to let them know I was taking the day off. My muscles and back were sore due to tightening my muscles and gripping the steering wheel, bracing my body for the impact. One of my coworker friends lived near me and when she heard about the accident immediately left work and arrived at my doorstep. Mary Ellen wasn't taking no for an answer and told me she was driving me to a doctor or the hospital—my choice. Doing nothing was not an option. Since Mary Ellen was insistent on me seeing a doctor, I asked her to take me to my chiropractor. My primary care physician had been out on disability, and I wasn't sure he was back. The chiropractor had worked with me for several years, he knew about my previous brain injury, and I completely trusted him.

When I shared with my chiropractor what happened, he told me I needed to get to my doctor or the emergency room to be treated, as my eyes were glassy and unresponsive, my speech was slurred, and I was not making sense. I am so lucky to have people in my life who take such good care of me. I went to see the recovering medical doctor, and Mary Ellen drove me to his office. He diagnosed me as having another concussion, this time on top of my already existing brain injury.

My poor head and brain. It has gone through so much over the years, but with each experience I learned to trust and lean on God even more to get me through these experiences. I never became bitter or blamed God for anything. I took each one as an opportunity to grow in my faith and share with others how God carried me through.

These stories are just some examples of how my faith muscles were strengthened, how each journey led to learning more about

God's grace and faithfulness, and how He never left my side. I look at each of these experiences as opportunities to share with others how God can carry you through during those valley times. The Bible teaches us we *walk through the valleys*. We don't stay there.

> *Yea, though I walk through the valley of the shadow of death...for You are with me. [Psalm 23:4) (NKJV)]*

Through my stories you can see how I have been touched directly by God and experienced many miracles. I pray my experiences will provide you with the strength to stand firm in your challenges. By trusting God, you will experience your own miracles.

CHAPTER 12

What Did I Learn?

I believed God had been preparing me my entire life to live as a brain injury survivor and to ultimately walk as a healed child of God. I also believe He was preparing me for my next journey, sharing my stories on healing, how to stand firm and walk by faith.

When I look back over these years and the documentation I've kept of my different experiences, I can see how much I have grown. Each experience tested as well as stretched my faith and prepared me to eventually step out in boldness and share God's miracles with others. How else could a shy young girl whose face turned bright red when someone asked her a question have blossomed into a young woman who now speaks in front of audiences sharing how Jesus healed her brain and body?

As I referenced previously, the Bible mentions how we go through valleys. It never says we stay in the valley, but go *through* them. While at the time of each experience I felt I would never get through them, I learned I always did because of God's help and guidance. Before these challenges, I never really knew God was alongside me. I thought He was somewhere out there in space. But now I know what I felt so strongly during those times was His presence. He had been right with me through each of these experiences and had never left my side.

Before my brain injury, what I was attracted to, and what drove me, was status and power. Growing up I figured out how to do everything myself. There wasn't much I felt I couldn't do from sports to school to my working environment. I loved climbing the corporate ladder, being the go-to person who had all the answers and a top performer on my job, winning trivia games, and being someone in charge and in control. Nothing was too difficult for me to handle even if I had never done it before. I don't feel it was ego. It was more like tremendous confidence in my own ability to do something or the aptitude to quickly learn. I always strived to be the best at whatever challenge I took on.

However, after a lifetime of success in sports, school, and my career, I became prideful, believing all these successes were because of my own ability. It was only after my brain injury and turning my life over to God I realized these successes were because of God's favor in my life.

When I look back on these times, I realize those feelings and personal passions that drove me distracted me from God and took on an idol type of worship. I had put my trust in me and my ability and performance and never relied on God or included Him in my day-to-day life. Don't get me wrong. He was a huge part of my life, but He was only a part of it. He wasn't my whole life. There is a big difference. When He is part of your life, He only hovers in the back of your mind. You make *some* time for Him, mostly on Sundays or maybe a few minutes in the morning or at night to say a quick prayer. However, when God is fully in your life, He is put first and consulted on everything encountered in life and becomes the central figure in all your thoughts and actions. Through these journey experiences, I learned to depend on God for everything, including breathing at times. He was never far from my thoughts.

Now as I approach work or anything else for that matter, I put my faith and trust in Him and relax in Jesus's arms instead of trying to do everything in my own strength. This relaxing rest provides you with an incredible peace, enabling you to handle whatever is thrown at you. You learn it is easier to trust in Jesus and ask for His guidance than to spend time worrying about making a decision you are faced with. Being a perfectionist and someone who analyzed every thought because I never wanted to make a wrong decision, putting my faith in Jesus helped me to calm down and know I couldn't go wrong if I followed His lead.

When I look back over these last several years, I've learned so much about God, not only from a factual perspective but also from a personal viewpoint. It has been great reading the Bible and studying the Old Testament; however, what has been an even greater experience has been meeting God through His son, Jesus.

Seeing Before Believing

My faith muscles grew, and my various understandings from the scriptures increased. Soon, my head knowledge moved to my heart, which then turned to belief in God's promises for my healing. But I also believe you need to see, or visualize, yourself healed before you are healed.

For example, in the years living with the brain injury, my dreams portrayed me as having a disability. I never saw myself well in my dreams. For instance, I couldn't walk fast or even run in them. When I awoke in the mornings and remembered my dreams, I saw myself as someone sick and disabled.

Here's the important point. Eventually, I started to see myself healthy in my dreams, active, and not sick or disabled. I can recall actually running across a street in a dream and knew it was a prediction of what was to come. Once my subconscious started to change, I believe something inside of me changed as well. I don't know the timing of all of this, but the outcome is the same—I am walking as a healed and whole person again, not just in my dreams. This experience was a kind of positive faith change. When I turned to God even more and believed his scriptural promises, I found myself walking in reality as a healed and whole person again, not just in a dream.

I had to believe and have faith *before* I was healed. Even Jesus, in Matthew 13:58, could do no miracles in his own town because the people's unbelief was so strong. One's mind-set must change and be open to miracles. Doubt and unbelief are limitations and block us from seeing and believing in God's healing power.

As I mentioned, many of my victories and attempts to overcome my problems came in my RAV4, my baby, my favorite car. I felt so close to God while I rode in that car. It carried me through many trials and triumphs over the years. I purchased it five years after I sustained the brain injury and kept it until the last accident when it was totaled. I had a hard time watching it being towed away feeling my miracles were being carried away as well. I had to quickly turn my thoughts back to God who performed the miracles, not the place where the miracles took place.

My Secret Place

Psalm 91 mentions a secret place to commune with God, *He who dwells in the secret place of the Most High shall abide under the shadow of the Almighty* (NKJV). I believe my secret place was my 2000 Toyota RAV4.

Inside that car He gave me creative ideas, answers to my questions, and even a giant rainbow when I was driving to a Wednesday night service and needing help dealing with a severe migraine and lightning bolts flashing in both eyes along with pain in my eyes and head. I reached out to God when I had been asked to say the prayer at a friend's wedding, something I had never done before, and didn't know what to say or how to even write a prayer. God gave me the entire prayer while I drove. Being in my car always felt safe to me, a place where I felt God's presence. God meets us where we are, and He met me in my RAV4.

My RAV4 was probably crushed somewhere, but I would like to believe someone replaced the damaged parts and has it. I hope that person is spending time with God and experiencing His incredible presence in the car. For me, I've found a new secret place. God blessed me with a new and bigger car with fancy gadgets in which I'm expecting even more incredible miracles.

My experiences with God over these years have been an incredible journey of learning. I have grown so much, my faith muscles are stronger, and my love for the Lord is even deeper. What I went through was far from easy. When I hear the amazement of others as I share my experiences, I recognize how challenging those times were and typically say, "I wouldn't wish this on my worst enemy." However, I don't think I'd want to trade in what God has done in my life.

Psalm 23 says, *Even when I walk through the darkest valley, I will not be afraid, for you are close beside me* (NAS).

To me, the important word is "through." It doesn't say we stay in the valley. While many times I thought I would never get out, I can tell you honestly, leaving the valley and seeing all God has done and is still doing in my life, this journey has definitely been worth taking.

My hope is that my stories have motivated you to stand firm and strong in your faith so you too can be touched by God and experience your own miracles.

HEALING SCRIPTURES

Isaiah 53: 4–5	Yet it was our weaknesses he carried; it was our sorrows that weighed him down. And we thought his troubles were a punishment from God, a punishment for his own sins! But he was pierced for our rebellion, crushed for our sins. He was beaten so we could be whole. He was whipped so we could be healed (NLT).
Isaiah 55:11	It is the same with my word. I send it out, and it always produces fruit. It will accomplish all I want it to, and it will prosper everywhere I send it (NLT).
Psalm 30:2	O *LORD* my God, I cried to you for help, and you restored my health (NLT).
Psalm 103:2–3	Let all that I am praise the LORD; may I never forget the good things he does for me. He forgives all my sins and heals all my diseases (NLT).
Proverbs 4:20–22	My child, pay attention to what I say. Listen carefully to my words. Don't lose sight of them. Let them penetrate deep into your heart, for they bring life to those who find them, and healing to their whole body (NLT).

Matthew 8:17	This fulfilled the word of the Lord through the prophet Isaiah, who said, "He took our sicknesses and removed our diseases" (NLT).
Mark 5:34	And he said to her, "Daughter, your faith has made you well. Go in peace. Your suffering is over" (NLT).
Mark 11:24	I tell you, you can pray for anything, and if you believe that you've received it, it will be yours (NLT).
Romans 10:10	For it is by believing in your heart that you are made right with God, and it is by confessing with your mouth that you are saved (NLT).
Romans 10:17	So faith comes from hearing, that is, hearing the Good News about Christ (NLT).
1 Peter 2:24	He personally carried our sins in his body on the cross so that we can be dead to sin and live for what is right. By his wounds you are healed. (NLT)

ABOUT THE AUTHOR

Donna Jones has always wanted to help people even as a young girl growing up in New Jersey. Over the years, she's volunteered her time with many organizations and even participated in numerous walks. Never would she believe one day, her friends and coworkers would be walking and raising money for her charity.

In 1995, Donna's world changed when she sustained a traumatic brain injury. After many years of traditional medicine and a deeper focus on her faith, Donna began her long journey toward recovery.

Donna shares her incredible journey in her first book: *From Night to Light: My Brain Injury Journey from Despair to Hope, Faith, and Joy.*

In her book, she explains what it was like living with a brain injury and the challenges she faced, getting the help to live in mainstream society, and ultimately how she overcame to live a victorious life. Donna's able to include some funny stories she remembers as well as ones provided to her by friends and family.

Healing has naturally become a huge part of her journey, and she is passionate about helping others through their challenges. Donna is one of the co-founders of a ministry called Healing Is For Everyone providing mentoring, teaching, and motivational speaking. For more information on Donna's ministry or to contact her directly, visit her web site at www.healingis4everyone.com.

CPSIA information can be obtained
at www.ICGtesting.com
Printed in the USA
LVHW101454250922
729231LV00004B/136

9 781642 995107